The
Battle of Flodden
Why & How

Clive Hallam-Baker

The Battle of Flodden Why & How

Published by The Remembering Flodden Project
www.flodden.net

© Clive Hallam-Baker 2012

Images (except otherwise shown) © The Remembering Flodden
Project, © Clive Hallam-Baker

First published 2012

ISBN 978 0 9573313 0 3

This book has been funded and supported by The National Lottery
through the Heritage Lottery Fund

Supported by

 The National Lottery®
through the Heritage Lottery Fund

 heritage
lottery fund

To the memory of
The Brave of Both Nations

Contents

List of Illustrations

Maps

Tables

Photographs, and stills from the DVD "The Battle of Flodden - Then & Now" by courtesy of Borderlands Fims

Interpretation board graphics by The Osprey Co. Coldstream, www.signsbynature.co.uk

How to Use this Book

The Battle of Flodden – Why and How? is written so that it can be read in several different ways. The first two sections give a brief glimpse into the way of life and the way of conducting war in late medieval times. This includes descriptions of the main protagonists at Flodden, the weapons that were available to them, and the ways that they were expected to be used.

The main section tells the story of why and how the Battle of Flodden came to be fought in an isolated and sparsely populated part of the Borderlands. It is not written as a history, but rather as a story condensed from a range of accounts of the Battle that date from 1513 up to modern times. The Battle is described in detail, with special reference being given to the topography of the Battlefield. It shows how some features of the site, that are still visible today, can be used to explain the turn of events of September 9th 1513. This section ends with the consequences of the Battle and how it shaped lives and the affairs of nations.

The next two sections are meant to be read on the Battlefield itself.

The Flodden Battlefield Trail is written from the point of view of combatants and describes the action and the dread, and perhaps relief, that they would have felt as battle progressed. The story is told first from the perspective of an English billman as you walk, starting at the Flodden Monument, along the Battlefield Trail.

It continues with the perception of the Battle from the Scottish position on Branxton Hill, describing how a soldier would have witnessed the changing fortunes of war, and how the topography and ground conditions rendered his 18 ft. long pike virtually useless.

The wider view of Flodden is then given in a descriptive tour as you walk, cycle or drive along the roads that encompass the Battlefield.

Each section is complete in itself, without reference to preceding or following sections. Some repetition is therefore inevitable, but this was considered to be preferable to flicking backwards and forwards through the book for the complete story. To help further with this, larger versions of the maps in this book can be downloaded from www.flodden.net

Acknowledgements

Writing this book was made possible only with the help of many people. First mention must go to James Nuttall and Michael Barnett; James for his invaluable expertise with all things electronic, Michael for his advice on arranging the book for printing, and both for their good humour as a semblance of order emerged from a jumble of text and photographs. I would like to thank Esmond and Isabelle Roney, for their support and for persuading me to start the book in the first place. Thanks are due to Kevin Malloy, Alison Standing, Barbara Nuttall and the many others who have walked or driven and checked routes and directions, or have proof read and corrected successive drafts of the book.

Members of the Glendale Local History Society and the Towton Battlefield Society have given valuable help by listening to ideas and reminding me about topics that I had missed. A special mention must be made of the late Peter Algar for sharing his knowledge and enthusiasm, and for linking the two great historic sites of Towton and Flodden.

Last, but by no means least, I must thank my wife, Angela, for her patience, and for putting up with months of books, paper, clutter and computers on the dining room table.

Flodden Monument

Introduction

As with all important episodes in history many accounts of the Battle of Flodden have been written. There are at least fifty versions in print, and no doubt more will appear during coming months as we approach the 500th anniversary of the Battle in September 2013. These accounts of the Battle contain many and varied theories as to what happened on that fateful day, and give a range of different reasons for the outcome. The numbers of casualties, the size and positions of the opposing armies vary greatly, and it is difficult to know which may be nearest to the truth. What must be remembered is that history is written by the victor in order that the success may appear the greater. Also it is virtually impossible to describe in accurate detail a battle even if you are there, because there is so much confusion and interaction that one person's perception may be completely different from that of a foe or even a closely placed compatriot.

Because of the discrepancy in the estimates of the size of the armies, any numbers used in describing the conflict are open to question, and, although I have in places used figures to quantify the size of the constituent parts of the opposing forces, these should be considered more as ratios than of actual numbers of combatants.

So what are my reasons for writing this book? I make no claims to being an historian; perhaps my only qualification is that I have lived in Branxton, on the actual Battlefield of Flodden, and have walked with my brace of Labradors across these fields of conflict almost daily these past 28 years. In doing so I have gained an intimate knowledge of the ground and how it is affected by weather and the seasons. Perhaps, as with the varied accounts of the Battle, my perception of what happened and how the day evolved has changed over the years, but the basics stay fixed in my mind and only the detail changes. I have given talks about the Battle, and have conducted guided walks over the ground, and almost every time a question has been asked, or an observation made which puts a new light on some aspects of the Battle. Every time I believe that I have an indisputable fact about Flodden, a note in a book, a comment from a visitor, a detail about the armaments or armour, adds that particle of doubt and starts the thinking process all over again.

Why then is the story of Flodden so evocative? Flodden did not change a ruling dynasty as happened at Hastings and Bosworth, but a ruling monarch, King James IV of Scotland died here, and an English family, the Howards, rose to prominence in the land, and history would most certainly have been different had the day been won by Scotland. Flodden was the result of the ambitions of a young Henry VIII, a campaign against France, and the incompatibility of two treaties that forced James IV to take up arms. Flodden was a duel between an impetuous monarch and an experienced septuagenarian military commander. It became a contest of tactics and manoeuvres, and the outcome was decided partly by the different armaments used by the two opposing sides, and also by an unexpected element, the ground conditions on the critical part of the Battlefield.

In spite of the heading of the first chapter, this book is not intended to be yet another history of the Battle of Flodden. Rather it is written as a guide, and a description both of the Battlefield where the final conflict occurred, and of the surrounding area and the places that also form a vital part of this intriguing and fateful episode in history. This book looks at the Battle of Flodden from different perspectives, first as a conventional narrative, secondly as if you were a soldier on the field of battle, and thirdly as you drive along the roads around the Battlefield.

This is a story of the causes and reasons for the success and failure, the triumph and despair that led to the deaths of a King and perhaps fourteen thousand soldiers in this quiet and isolated corner of late medieval England. It is based both on the early accounts of the Battle, and on more recent evidence and opinion. Also considered is the topography, and how the ground itself might have determined the outcome as much as the tactics of the military commanders.

This book will guide you over the Battlefield as we now understand it, and it will also point the way to other sites across Northumberland, the Borderlands and further afield, all of which are essential parts of the Flodden story. It may well come to pass that new discoveries will be made, either through archaeology or research into ancient documentation and correspondence, that will change our view of the Battle of Flodden. This has happened recently at

Bosworth, where archaeologists, metal detectorists and the Battlefields Trust have uncovered cannon balls and artefacts, the discovery of which has in effect "moved" the main part of the Battle several miles, but in the process have given rise to a much better understanding of the events that saw Henry VII take the throne of England and give rise to the start of the Tudor dynasty.

The theatre of operations of Flodden covers a much larger area than the few fields near Branxton of the actual conflict. I will try to describe the larger picture and the manoeuvring that took place over the preceding days as the commanders of the two armies jockeyed for position, trying to gain advantage before the climax of Battle on September 9th.

I expect that this book will raise more questions than it provides answers; that is the nature of battles and of Flodden in particular. But I hope that in the process you will look at the landscape and work out where it might have been possible for an army to pass, for guns to be placed and for thousands of armed men to assemble for the fray. Depending on the weather, you might be able to judge for yourself the likely ground conditions of half a millennium past, and if it would have been possible for ranks of armed men to cross, or where a defensive line of archers or billmen might have been of most use.

Flodden is the story of monarchs who found cause for war, of commanders who controlled the battle, and of the armaments and tactics they employed. But it is

4

also the story of the ordinary men who did the fighting, and of the ground over which the battle was fought. Every aspect of Flodden begs a question, and every question has a multitude of answers.

Perhaps the first question to be asked is - why is it called the Battle of Flodden and not the Battle of Branxton?   The battle was fought at Branxton and indeed was, in official English documents, originally called the Battle of Branxton, or the Battle of Branxton Moor.

The answer to this question and many others may appear in this book.

Or you may have your own ideas!

Clive Hallam-Baker
Branxton 2012

A Very Brief History

The Borderlands

The Northumberland of the early 1500s was recently described as once having been England's Afghanistan. Most certainly, compared to the more progressive parts of Tudor England, it was a wild, uncivilised and ungovernable place where the rule of law reached only tenuously. The total population of England was less than three million, and Northumberland was amongst the most sparsely peopled counties in the country. A similar situation existed north of the Border with Edinburgh being a centre for artistic, commercial and scientific advancement, with progress in the Borders lagging far behind.

After taking the English Throne at the Battle of Bosworth in 1485, the first Tudor King, Henry VII, had fostered, at least on the surface, friendly relations between the two nations and, for a few decades, the Borderlands had been relatively quiet. Henry had secured the marriage of his daughter Margaret to King James IV of Scotland and had instigated treaties to ensure peace between the two nations. But the inevitable cross-border incursions and raids, by the Scots and English alike, made this area less secure and prosperous than it might otherwise have been. Raids were intermittent and ranged between small scale forays by parties of Reivers, to larger invasions headed by local warlords or even royalty.

In this ferocious, yet neglected and sparsely populated

Border area the most important town was the port of Berwick-upon-Tweed. In the years between 1018 and 1482 Berwick-upon-Tweed had been subjected to attack and siege on many occasions and had changed hands between England and Scotland no fewer than thirteen times, but, despite these disturbances, by the early 1500s Berwick-upon-Tweed was a major strategic port and town of significant size. It was defended by substantial perimeter walls, artillery and a permanent garrison of about 600 and was by now firmly in English hands. Even then Berwick remained independent, with legal documents referring to it as being of the Kingdom of England, but not within it. The return of Berwick to Scotland must have been a great temptation and a potential valuable prize for James IV and Scotland.

A situation that remains unchanged to this day!

The number of castles, bastles, towers and fortified houses in the Border region is an indication of the insecurity of the times, and the isolated towns and villages on both sides of the Tweed were at the mercy of even small raiding parties.

Agriculture was very much the mainstay of the Border economy, and livestock and crops were not only vulnerable to depredation from raiders from across the Border, but might also be confiscated by a "friendly" army foraging for supplies for troops and horses. If this happened, farm rents would not be forthcoming, and landowners suffered along with their tenants.

Records show that the village of Branxton was no stranger to Scottish raids and suffered destruction and deprivation several times in the years leading to Flodden. Branxton was destroyed in 1496 when James IV, as a precursor to his 1513 Flodden campaign, led a major raid into Northumberland. Again in the summer of 1513, before the main Scottish incursion, Branxton was once more ravaged during the Douglas "Ill Raid". One can imagine the dismay of the villagers of Branxton in August 1513 as news spread of a full Scottish army crossing the Tweed. They would either have waited in trepidation, or, more likely, packed their meagre belongings and left the area until more settled times promised.

In short, life in the Borderlands was tough, even by the harsh standards of medieval England. Today Northumberland still remains relatively sparsely populated. Administrative areas of the County Council and Parliamentary Constituency are amongst the largest in area in the UK, and yet have the smallest number of constituents. Perhaps this is the legacy of the troubled times of half a millennium past.

Henry VIII, King of England

The year 1509 saw a young King Henry VIII accede to the throne of England. As a second son, Henry had not expected to become King, but the early death in 1502 of Arthur, his elder brother, and seven years later the death of his father Henry VII, pushed the unprepared eighteen year old Henry into this exalted, yet unexpected position. At this stage the Tudor claim

Henry VIII circa 1509
This portrait depicts Henry aged 18
around the time he became King

Catherine of Aragon
Henry's first wife

to the throne was not secure. Henry's father had, in effect, usurped the throne by defeating the Yorkist Richard III at the Battle of Bosworth, and Henry himself, judging by contemporary portraits, appeared to be a rather weak and callow character. But in fact Henry was made of much sterner stuff than his looks might suggest. He was now married to Catherine of Aragon, his late brother's widow, and had dispensed with the services of many of his father's councillors, replacing them with advisers more to his own way of thinking. Henry was looking to bolster his status amongst his fellow European monarchs and leaders. At home he also needed to secure his, and the Tudor dynasty's position, amongst the wider populace of England. The quickest way to achieve this was for him to gain military victory on the battlefield; popularity and political kudos would inevitably follow. To this end Henry decided to embark on another episode of the ever popular English sport of fighting the French.

Henry's pretext for war was that he had a just and rightful claim to the French throne, and at this point in time the situation on mainline Europe afforded him an ideal opportunity to pursue his ambition. France under King Louis XII had invaded parts of northern Italy, and a military consortium was assembled to counter this French belligerence. This military group, the Holy League, which included Spain, Pope Julius II and the Holy Roman Emperor, made ready for war against France. Henry eagerly seized the chance to join the Holy League. He immediately began to raise an army, gathered largely from the southern counties of England. He called the campaign his

Grand Undertaking, and the Great and Good of the land rushed enthusiastically to join the operation that would increase English holdings around Calais, the last remaining English possession on the continent. This was to be the first step in Henry's ambition to renew the English claim to the Throne of France which dated back to Henry V and Agincourt.

Henry VIII was fortunate in his preparations for war. His father had been careful with money, many would say that he had been downright miserly, but the coffers of England were full, and the young King had a plentiful supply of that fundamental requisite for war, hard cash for supplies, and for soldiers' pay.

In late June 1513 Henry's Grand Undertaking began. Accompanied by eager members of the English nobility, Henry embarked for Calais, taking the best and most modern military equipment available, and an army of indented soldiers. There was one notable omission from the Dukes, Lords and Earls who went to France; the ageing Thomas Howard, Earl of Surrey remained in England, smarting that he was to miss the campaign.

But Henry had other plans for the Earl of Surrey. Trouble from across the northern Border was expected and Henry left his wife Catherine of Aragon as Regent in control of England during his absence and he installed Surrey as Lord Lieutenant of the Northern Marches with orders to "trust not the Scots" and to prepare to resist invasion.

James IV, King of Scotland

James IV is known as Scotland's Renaissance King. Patron of the arts and charismatic leader of a spectacular Royal Court, James was the builder of a powerful Navy and procurer of some of the most modern arms and artillery in Europe.   He was held in high regard throughout Scotland and most importantly, greatly respected by Clan Chiefs of the Highlands, Islands and Lowlands.

James IV of Scotland was married to England's Henry VIII's sister, Margaret. The marriage was cemented by the Treaty of Perpetual Peace which bound the two Kingdoms in harmony on pain of excommunication for the aggressor.   In spite of the frequency of cross-border incursions by both sides, this arrangement had worked reasonably well during the lifetime of Henry VII. But the ambitions in France of the young successor Henry VIII put James in an impossible situation. Scotland and France were bound by The Auld Alliance, a long-standing mutual defensive pact that promised aid should either be attacked by England. James had to decide which treaty to uphold.

By 1513, after skirmishes at sea and diplomatic exchanges, relations with England had deteriorated. Inducements by way of gold, arms and military advisors from the French King Louis XII, and gifts of jewellery and billets-doux from Anne, his Queen, ensured that James chose to uphold the French connection rather than the ties with his brother-in-law. This provided little difficulty for the Scots as for

James IV of Scotland

Margaret Tudor
James' wife and sister to Henry
VIII

centuries they had traditionally taken advantage of the absence of a King of England to mount raids across the River Tweed. At Queen Anne's behest James was persuaded to "take one yard of English land" and so open up a second front in the hope of forcing Henry to send at least part of his attacking army back home from France to defend England's northern Border.

James was held in such high regard that by July 24th he was able to assemble a feudal army from all parts of Scotland, thus uniting his country in its dispute with neighbouring England. The muster was at Boroughmuir outside Edinburgh. Some estimates put the number of soldiers as high as 100,000, but this figure is unrealistic and a more reasonable estimate would be about 40,000.

The formality of a declaration of war did not occur until Henry was fully engaged in his Continental foray when, on August 11th 1513, Scottish Lyon Herald was received by Henry at the English camp outside the besieged French town of Therouanne which lies some miles to the south of Calais. Two days after this the Douglas raid into England was ambushed 5 miles north of Wooler at Milfield, as the Scottish raiding party made its way home laden with plunder, cattle and the spoils of war. Perhaps it was an omen, because many Scots were killed or taken prisoner and the incursion earned the name of the "Ill Raid".

The assembled Scottish army at Boroughmuir was ready to march by August 19th and, after gathering additional forces from the Lowlands, reached

Coldstream on the north bank of the River Tweed ready to invade an undefended northern England.

Thomas Howard, The Earl of Surrey

Thomas Howard, the Earl of Surrey was in his seventies, and was crippled with arthritis. At first glance he seemed to be an unlikely choice for such a vitally important military command. He had fought and been wounded at the Battle of Bosworth, where his father, who had recently been created the first Duke of Norfolk, had been killed. Unfortunately for the Howard family, they had fought on the losing side and, after the death of Richard III, the Dukedom had been rescinded, and Thomas Howard, rather than becoming the second Duke of Norfolk, was imprisoned in the Tower of London. However during the ensuing years Howard worked his way back into favour, first with Henry VII, and then with the new king, Henry VIII. He became a trusted and invaluable advisor to the Throne of England and his military expertise and command ability was greatly valued.

By 1513 the Howard family fortunes were again in the ascendancy. But Surrey was not in favour with all those who held power, and long standing disagreements with Wolsey, Henry's influential Chancellor, prevented his inclusion in the King's prestigious and glamorous French campaign.

Surrey's anger must have been tempered by the responsibility and opportunity offered on his appointment as Lord Lieutenant of the Northern

Marches and he immediately started preparations for war.   He commandeered ships to transport supplies to Newcastle, mobilised 500 retainers from his own estates and sent notice to nobles and landowners in the northern counties of Lancashire, Cheshire, Yorkshire, Cumberland, Westmorland and Northumberland to raise levies to form a second English army, and to march north to counter the inevitable Scottish incursion.

Surrey must have been aware that this was the best chance for him to gain glory and to secure the future of the Howard family.   This was an opportunity not to be missed, squandered or mismanaged.

Thomas Howard, The Earl of Surrey

The Weapons and Tactics of War

By 1513 warfare and fighting had, in many ways, changed very little from ancient times. Indeed the Roman General, Vegetius' writings, *De re militari* had become the text book for infantry warfare and essential reading for Kings and all military commanders. This, and Christine de Pizan's *Deeds of Arms and Chivalry*, set out advice on how to engage in battle, and the rules that were to be followed in war.

The outcome of battle largely depended upon many factors, but the final outcome usually depended on the mêlée of close quarter hand to hand fighting. Here the extent of the killing area was dependent largely on the range of hand-held weaponry and the numbers of combatants who could be entrapped within this space. Certainly missiles had always been used in battle, but their use was to drive the infantry masses into a more confined area where they could be more easily dealt with. If an enemy could be forced into a compacted defensive posture by gunfire or arrow storms raining in from English longbows, their closely packed ranks would make movement virtually impossible and suffocation would be a peril equal to that of incoming missiles.

Even in medieval times there was an ongoing arms race. Armour was developed to protect against hand weapons and missiles, and these in turn were improved to counteract such developments. Armour was expensive; the best was very expensive and only the very rich could afford this sort of protection. At

English Billhook versus Scotish Pike

English Soldier

Helmet

Quilted leather jerkin

erhaps ome hain mail

8ft (2.4m) billhook, possibly fashioned from everyday hedging tool.

18 foot (5.5m) pike

Scottish Soldier

Wooden targe (shield)

Heavy Scottish Gun
These cannon weighed up to 4 tonnes and each required a team of 36 oxen to move.

Flodden the best armour would provide defence against arrows, but the common soldiers of both sides would have to make the best of whatever was available.

There was no standardisation of equipment, offensive weaponry or defensive armour. Helmets and pieces of body armour were begged, borrowed, stolen, handed down or found on battlefields and used, repaired, and used again. Body armour might be a leather jerkin or an arming jack made of layers of linen or padded with wool. The better jacks were reinforced by metal plates sewn into the fabric. It is sometimes argued that arrows from the longbow could not pierce plate armour. The opposite view is also put, and evidence is confusing and contradictory. The most likely truth is that some arrows would pierce some plate armour, and others would not, all depending on the quality of the materials, the skill of the maker and the luck of the protagonists.

Artillery had been used in battle long before Flodden. Recent archaeology has uncovered evidence at Bosworth, fought in 1485, that shows significant use of guns during the Battle. Guns had been used as siege weapons at Harfleur in 1415 prior to Agincourt, but Flodden was almost certainly the first time in the British Isles that battle commenced with a more formalised artillery exchange.

The Scots

The Scottish artillery train consisted of seventeen large to medium calibre guns plus a range of smaller pieces. It included some of the most modern cast bronze ordnance of the times, with the heaviest guns firing an iron ball of up to 66lbs weight. Some of the guns fired a rounded stone ball and the maximum range of the Scottish guns varied from about 1100 to 2000 yards. The downside of using this heavy artillery was the necessity to employ large teams of gunners, blacksmiths, drovers etc. for each gun. The heaviest guns each needed a team of thirty-six oxen, and progress was limited to a maximum of about two miles per hour. Also needed were hundreds of horses, panniers and carts to carry round shot and powder.

The recoil on the heavy guns was massive, and they had to be dug into prepared emplacements both for defence against incoming missiles, and also so that, after every shot, they could be re-sited, reloaded and re-aimed with minimum difficulty. The heavy ball fired from these large calibre guns had a relatively slow muzzle velocity and would, in effect, be lobbed at the target over a steep parabolic curve. It therefore arrived on target at a steep angle, and although it could cause casualties, damage would be limited to the very small area where it fell because the ball would tend to bury itself in the ground rather than bounce and cause further havoc.

There was a further problem with these heavy guns. They were muzzle loaders, were slow to reload and fire, and they overheated quickly. Estimates for the firing rate of these guns vary from once every twenty minutes or so, to more than an hour between shots, with a maximum of just a few (less than ten) shots per day. Essentially these were siege guns and their use in field operations was to prove to be questionable.

For James' 1513 campaign the pike was to be the chosen infantry weapon. The pike was an 18ft long lance with a lethal steel spike at the tip, and had been supplied by the thousand by James' French allies. This weapon had proved to be invincible on the Continent; first used by the Swiss, it had also been used to great advantage by other nations. Success with the pike depended on several factors; discipline was essential and training in its use was crucial to success. The topography and ground conditions of the battle ground also had to be taken into consideration when using pikes in closely packed massed ranks.

Soldiers in pike formations, or schiltrons, had to keep in close formation. To be effective they needed to form an unbroken front of deadly steel spikes, to keep the line of advance straight, and at all costs to keep moving forward. The varying steepness of the slopes and the patchy existence of boggy ground on, and below Branxton Hill, made it very poor pike country. To add to these difficulties, the Scots had only a very short time in which to train and perfect the required skills and discipline to make them a successful fighting force of pikemen.

It is uncertain how the pike schiltrons were formed up for battle at Flodden. Squares, line abreast several ranks deep, arrow head formations are all possibilities. The most likely formation however was for a wide front to be presented, say 300 to 400 across and 20 or so ranks deep. What is agreed is that the schiltrons moved into battle with the Scottish Left first to engage, followed by the Centre division and lastly the division on the Right flank. The effect of massed pikes has been likened to the use of tank formations. Dependent on movement and the shock of impact, the schiltrons had to preserve their momentum. If stopped, the 18 foot long pike became an encumbrance rather than a usable weapon and hand weapons such as swords, daggers and axes would have to be used.

The Scots did have their more traditional weapons; the claymore, a two-handed brute of a sword, and the battle-axe, were favourites for close quarter fighting. The pike men, especially the front ranks, were supplied with steel armour, but others further to the rear were less well protected. Archers were present in the Scottish ranks, but not in the same numbers, nor with the same effectiveness as in the English forces.

This Scottish army was probably the largest army ever to be mustered north of the Border. James was able to draw men from all parts of Scotland and loyal Clan Chiefs brought soldiers from the Highlands, Islands and Lowlands to take up arms against the traditional foe to the south.

The English

By contrast to the impressive Scottish array of modern kit, and an army led by a King and Nobles from across Scotland, the English army was in effect a hastily assembled second team led by an over-the-hill Earl.

The guns that the Earl of Surrey had at his disposal were much less impressive than the state of the art weapons that James brought with him. All the best and most modern artillery had been taken by King Henry on his French Campaign, and Surrey had to make do with about eighteen small calibre field guns. These guns were made of wrought iron slats formed into a cylinder and held together by iron rings and hoops which were heat shrunk around the fabrication to form a barrel-like structure; possibly the origin of the name "gun barrel".

They fired a round shot made up of an iron cube cast round with lead to form a ball just larger than a golf ball, and weighing about 1lb. This ball was fired at high muzzle velocity and therefore would move on a flat trajectory, and on impact could split into small shards and cut a swathe through closely packed ranks of soldiers. Round shot of this type has been found on the Flodden Battlefield. These are similar to round shot brought up from the wreck of the Mary Rose at Portsmouth and dates them specifically to Tudor times.

The light English field guns, although they did not fire a comparable weight of shot to their Scottish counterparts, had several distinct advantages. They were easy to move and, on the day of Battle, had been man-hauled the eleven miles from Barmoor to Branxton. They were breach loaders and, the gunners being able to prepare and load several breach pieces at a time, the rate of fire was rapid, and far quicker than the Scottish guns. Manoeuvring and aiming were also quicker, and the high muzzle velocity and

Light English Field Gun - A Falconet
These guns fired a 1lb. iron cored lead ball slightly larger in size than a golf ball

5cm

flat trajectory of the ball ensured accuracy of shot. The composite nature of the iron core and lead covering of the ball added to its lethal effect. Firing uphill, the English had a large and yet closely packed target and their cannon balls had a devastating and demoralising effect on the Scots. The Scots were positioned well within the 1500 yard range of the English guns and would have taken heavy casualties.

The opening artillery exchange of Flodden was just the precursor to the main battle, but how were the English to defend against the massed ranks of pikes? For two centuries the English had relied on the longbow as their most important weapon of war. Archers were trained in its use from the age of seven, and practice at the archery butts was compulsory – even to the exclusion of football. Immense pride in their fighting prowess was taken by skilled archers, but in battle they did not depend entirely on their longbows. An archer also carried a short sword, a small diameter buckler shield, an eye-wateringly named ballock dagger and perhaps an archer's mell, a heavy lead bound wooden mallet for striking against heads or plate armour.

Upper body strength was paramount for an archer. The pull on the longbow could be up to 170 lbs, and the arrows had a killing range of over 250 yards. With a shooting rate of an arrow every six seconds, an archer could have five or six arrows in flight at any one time. Arrows were loosed together in flights of thousands, and the resulting arrow storms would cause havoc, casualties and deaths especially with packed ranks as targets. The technology developed for the production

The Medieval Archer
Trained from the age of seven

5cm

Arrowheads
Different heads for piearcing
plate armour, chain mail, or
causing flesh wounds

of arrows was highly advanced. Different arrowheads were made for different uses or targets; the bodkin for piercing armour, the long bodkin for chainmail, and others for flesh wounds. The arrow shafts were also shaped or tapered for greater effect, and goose feather fletching chosen and fixed to ensure that, similar to a rifle bullet, the arrow rotated in flight.

The other main weapon of the English was the billhook, which was little more than a modified hedging tool fixed onto the end of an 8 ft long ash pole. There was no set pattern for the billhook. This was not a standing army, and there was no standard issue of armaments to the levied soldiers. A billman would take his hedging hook or knife to the local blacksmith who might add a point and a couple of spikes and then, fixed to a longer handle, a simple agricultural tool was transformed into a fearsome and deadly weapon in the hands of an ordinary farm worker who had now become a levied soldier and fierce fighting man.

Other armaments carried by a billman might include sword, dagger, steel helmet and any armour or padded jacket that he could find, beg, borrow, steal or glean from the battlefield.

Lead arquebus balls have been found at Flodden indicating that early handguns were almost certainly used during the Battle. These however were not used in great numbers and it was quite some years before the use of firearms ousted longbows as the favoured distance weapon of the English. Compulsory training for archers remained until well into the reign of Elizabeth I, although it soon became quicker, easier and more practical to train potential conscript soldiers in the use of hand guns. Shot and firearms also quickly improved to become much better armour piercing weapons than arrows loosed from longbows.

Logistics

The science and practice of logistics changed very little right up to 1918 when mechanisation began to replace the horse. An army was comprised of more than just fighting men; it also needed probably an equal number of men, and women, in support. A vast number of draught animals, horses for riding and animals for food were also essential requirements. These, as well as the human contingent, all needed to be fed, and the transportation of fodder and provisions was a major consideration in moving an army. Anything that could not be gathered by foraging had to be carried.

Remaining in any one place was also a problem for an army. Medieval personal hygiene, by modern standards, left much to be desired and lice, parasites and latrines (or lack of) quickly led to disease, epidemic and the rapid reduction of an army as a fighting force.

Drinking water was not generally carried in bulk, but relying on stream or puddle water was dangerous and, if contaminated, was another source of sickness such as dysentery, typhoid fever or cholera. Supplies of small beer, made with boiled water or wine were essential requirements for the prevention of disease and if not carried in the baggage train, they had to be available either from a regular local source or by foraging.

Moving heavy equipment required teams of draught animals; the largest Scottish guns need thirty-two oxen to move them, whereas the light English guns were man-hauled to battle. Powder, shot and the myriad needs of artillery necessitated yet more carts, drivers, draught animals and fodder. The Scottish 18 foot long pikes were too unwieldy to be carried individually and these were also transported in carts, with the similar accoutrements.

Villagers and local people would dread the approach of an army, hostile or otherwise. The countryside was able to support and feed only a limited number of people and an advancing army would spell utter disaster for farmers, peasants and landowners alike. An invading hoard would pick the area clean by looting and pillaging Even paying for goods and food might lead to starvation for the indigenous population, and an offer to pay would probably remain as just an offer. A foraging army, foe or friendly, would pick the land clean, leaving a trail several miles wide to mark its passing. No wonder the Borderlands suffered during the years of raiding, dispute and war. At Flodden the Scots had occupied the area for a considerable time and would have laid waste to the land so that foraging was not an option for Surrey's advancing army.

Bulk supplies were delivered to the port of Newcastle as Surrey moved north, but land transport over the 50 or so miles to Flodden made further use of this port impracticable. The move to Barmoor, just a few miles from Berwick-upon-Tweed, shortened the English supply lines. This gave Surrey several options: he could simply lay siege to Flodden Hill and starve the Scots into surrender; or perhaps advance across the River Tweed and attack the Scottish Borderlands; or move further north and directly attack Scotland's capital city, Edinburgh. Either of the last two options would force James to move from Flodden Hill to defend his kingdom.

This change in logistical outlook, at a stroke, altered the strategic possibilities available to the Earl of Surrey. It also put King James in a quandary. Should he stay and fight an army who now have a distinct, and growing, advantage? Or should he withdraw across the River Tweed?

The Role of Women at Flodden

The general perception of medieval battles is that they are exclusively all male activities, but it is not so with the story of Flodden. Here, women played a vital part at every stage of the conflict.

Three Queens are prominent in the story of Flodden. Henry VIII's first wife Catherine of Aragon had been appointed as Regent in Henry's absence during his foray in France, and it was Catherine who oversaw Surrey's preparations to defend England's northern border. Catherine also had made contingency plans in case Surrey failed to shift the Scots from English land. She had raised and equipped an additional army, and was moving north in support of Surrey, but had reached only as far as Buckingham when news of Surrey's victory at Flodden reached her.

It must have been a severe blow to Henry's pride that, in spite of his longing for military kudos, Flodden was not to be his victory. Rather, as Regent, victory belonged to Catherine, a situation that must have rankled in later years when royal marital relationships turned sour.

King James IV of Scotland was married to Margaret, Henry VIII's elder sister, and part of the marriage agreement was the Treaty of Perpetual Peace between the two nations. Excommunication was to be the penalty for breaking the Treaty. It may be thought that Queen Margaret's loyalties would have been divided between her husband and brother, but there was bad feeling between the Tudor siblings because Henry had held back jewellery, part of his sister's dowry. In spite of this, the two still exchanged affectionate letters, and Margaret did her best to ease a deteriorating situation between the two countries. In the final analysis Margaret's loyalty was to her husband, King James and her adopted country, Scotland.

She and King James also fulfilled their duty by continuing a line of succession that would, just ninety years after the Battle of Flodden, ensure the union of the thrones of England and Scotland under James VI of Scotland who also became James I of England.

Queen Anne, wife of King Louis XII of France was instrumental in ensuring that James observed the

Auld Alliance rather than The Treaty of Perpetual Peace. She is reputed to have sent gifts of jewellery, and billets-doux to James cajoling him to take "one yard of English land". Military action would open a second front on England's northern border, and hopefully, force Henry to send some of his invading forces home from France and so relieve the pressure on France's overstretched armies.

James, with his feeling for gallantry and a reputation as a ladies' man, succumbed to Anne's entreaties and started preparations for war against his brother-in-law, and neighbour, England.

Lady Heron, chatelaine of Ford Castle is part of this account of Flodden. Her husband, Sir John Heron, owner of Ford Castle was held prisoner by the Scots as hostage for the murderous deeds of his half brother, The Bastard Heron. After taking Norham and Etal Castles, James next attacked Ford, and the story goes that Lady Heron detained James "in dalliance" to prevent the castle's destruction and to give Surrey's approaching army time to advance. There is little or no evidence as to the truth of these events, but it does make a good yarn and is now firmly set in folklore. Whatever the truth of this story, it did not work to Lady Heron's advantage. James burned Ford Castle to the ground and then moved to join his army on Flodden Hill where the Scots had constructed a well defended camp which was protected by a range of modern artillery.

A lady of high standing and reputation was Isabella

Hopringle, of Coldstream Priory. Of aristocratic background, she had forsaken the trappings of wealth and comfortable living to become Prioress at Coldstream. It was she who led her nuns onto the Battlefield of Flodden after the carnage had ceased to tend to the wounded and to gather bodies for Christian burial.

Armies of all countries are renowned for collecting camp followers of dubious moral standing. There are no records to prove this at Flodden, but we do know that some wives, and probably girlfriends did accompany their menfolk to the Battle. Two of the archers depicted and named in the stained glass windows of Middleton Church, Manchester took, or were taken by, their wives. They are named as "Thomas Cheetham and Wyfe and Edward Wylde and Wyfe".

Many wives and girlfriends would not trust their men to be in the company of the more traditional camp followers, and would insist that they be chaperoned to keep them from straying. Although in today's P.C. climate it is hardly acceptable to say, women were in fact needed at medieval army camps for domestic chores such as washing, cooking and general, but essential hygiene. Also, if things went well, an extra pair of hands might well be useful to help carry away valuable loot or gleanings from the battlefield.

A group of women who were highly valued after battle were "the wise women"; those women who had a special knowledge of herbs and their use in treating wounds and ailments. Sphagnum moss was used as an antiseptic balm and could prevent the fatal onset of sepsis or gangrene. Their knowledge of herbs could put the wise women at odds with barber surgeons and their brutal cut and saw methods. In following years, contrary to any form of reasoned justice some such women were brutally, undeservedly and most cruelly hanged as witches.

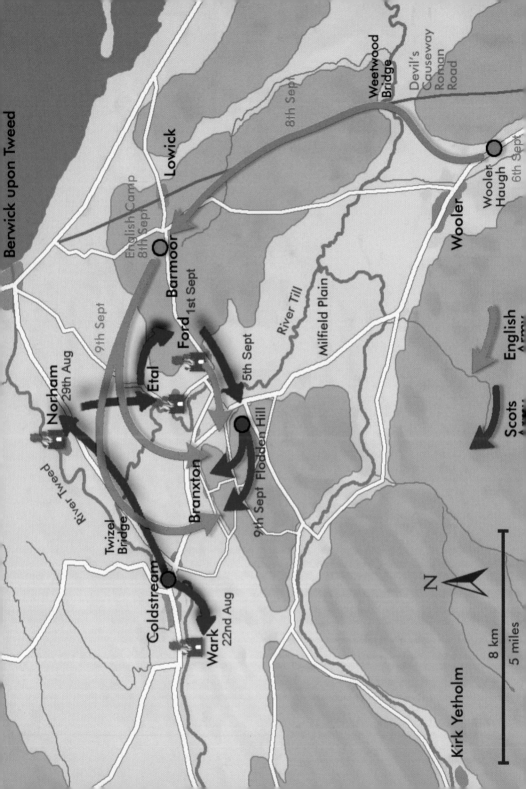

Berwick upon Tweed

Weetwood Bridge

Devil's Causeway Roman Road

8th Sept

Lowick

Wooler Haugh 6th Sept

Wooler

English Camp 8th Sept

Barmoor

Ford 1st Sept

River Till

Milfield Plain

English Army

9th Sept

Etal

5th Sept

Norham 29th Aug

Scots Army

Flodden Hill

Branxton

River Tweed

9th Sept

Twizel Bridge

Coldstream

Wark 22nd Aug

N

8 km

5 miles

Kirk Yetholm

Battle of Flodden or The Battle of Branxton Moor

The Build up to Flodden

August 22nd 1513 was the day that James IV of Scotland crossed the River Tweed with his army into an undefended northern England. A detachment was immediately sent to take Wark Castle which guarded a crossing point of the Tweed just to the west of Coldstream. The main body of the Scottish army assembled at Twizel Haugh, where James held his last Parliament to grant immunity from death taxes to the family of any soldier killed during the campaign. James then moved eastward along the Tweed to Norham where he laid siege to the better defended and much more substantial Norham Castle. Surrey and his growing army by this time had reached only as far as Pontefract in Yorkshire and posed no threat to the Scots. It was at Pontefract that Surrey received confirmation of the Scottish attack; news which stressed the urgency of the situation and quickened the pace of the growing English army.

The Scots besieged Norham Castle and used their heavy guns to blast its stone defences. Sir Richard Cholmeley, Captain of Norham Castle put up a brave defence until, out of ammunition, Norham was surrendered to the much larger attacking force. There is a story that Norham was betrayed by an English traitor who gave away details of the weaker parts of the Castle walls, and was rewarded for his efforts by later being hanged by the Scots. This episode is unlikely,

Map 1 - The Routes Of The Two Armies To Flodden   37

Norham Castle
Surrendered to the Scots after a 5 day seige

Defensive Walls, Berwick-upon-Tweed

but the fact that Norham surrendered before being destroyed perhaps indicates that the heavy Scottish guns were not as effective as has been suggested.

By the 29th of August the Scots controlled the River Tweed and all the possible crossing points from Norham to Wark, west of Coldstream.

They made no attempt to attack the well defended Berwick-upon-Tweed.

James now ventured deeper into enemy territory. Moving south along the River Till he took the poorly defended Etal Castle and then occupied the nearby, but stronger castle at Ford. This done, James had amply fulfilled Queen Anne of France's request to take one yard of English land.

Ford Castle fell to the Scots on September 1st. James remained here, but his army moved a further two miles to the south west. Here on the steep sided andesite outcrop known as Flodden Hill, the Scots set up their final camp and prepared their defences. On September 5th James burned Ford Castle to the ground and moved to the secure fortifications on Flodden Hill to await the arrival of the Earl of Surrey.

James set his guns to cover the expected approach of the English from the south across Milfield Plain and to cover a possible crossing point of the River Till. Recently investigations have been carried out on Flodden Hill, but to date little evidence of gun positions have been found, but indications of a fortified

Scottish camp at the very top of Flodden Hill have been uncovered. Many of the Scottish artillery pieces were heavy calibre guns designed for siege warfare and battering down defensive walls. They needed to be dug into secure gun emplacements, both for protection from incoming fire, and to enable quick repositioning and reloading. This requirement was to cause problems on the day of Battle.

Feeling that their camp was now secure, the Scots could only sit, and wait for the inevitable English response.

After marching northwards, through Pontefract, York, Durham and Newcastle, Surrey reached his final muster point at Bolton near Powburn, just a few miles from Alnwick. The English army now consisted of about twenty to twenty-five thousand fighting men. Here Surrey was joined by his elder son, the Lord Admiral who, with 1000 professional soldiers detached from the French campaign, had brought his Flagship, The Mary Rose, to Newcastle at the head of a supply fleet. But, because of storms, not all the supplies had arrived and the English position would soon become precarious as provisions ran short.

With the two armies assembled, and within communicating distance, the time had arrived to begin the formalities that would lead to battle. Surrey sent Herald Rouge Croix to the Scottish camp with the offer of battle on Friday September 9th. King James received Rouge Croix and agreed to Surrey's challenge. He contracted to engage in battle with the English

challenger and to this end would wait until noon on Friday September 9th.

Rather than let Surrey's Herald return with vital intelligence about the Scottish army, armaments and encampment, James held Rouge Croix prisoner, and sent his own Herald Islay with acceptance of Surrey's terms.

No quarter was offered by either side; a brutal encounter was now inevitable.

Surrey had secured his first objective, he had only limited supplies and September 9th was realistically the latest date on which his army would be fit for battle. On September 6th Surrey advanced to Wooler Haugh, about 9 miles to the south of the Scottish position on Flodden Hill. A derelict building known as Surrey House stands on a awkward kink in the road on the A697 a couple of miles south of Wooler, and marks the site where Surrey is reputed to have made his headquarters.

Wooler was firmly in English hands and was protected by a Tower and a garrison of 20. The Tower was located on the hill to the west of Church Street.

On the following day, September 7th, Rouge Croix returned to the English camp with unsettling, but vital intelligence for Surrey. He brought news of the fortified Scottish camp on Flodden Hill, and detailed information about guns, numbers and armaments.

Ford Castle
Destroyed by King James as he moved to Flodden Hill

Surrey House
One and a half miles south of Wooler, on the A697

Weetwood Bridge
The English army crossed the River Till here en route from Wooler to Barmoor

Surrey had expected to fight on the "flat, fair ground" of Milfield Plain and was dismayed to learn of the Scots' advantageous position on the high ground overlooking the north of the Plain. He immediately sent Rouge Croix back to suggest in the strongest possible terms that battle should indeed take place on the flat ground of Milfield Plain. King James was incensed at Surrey's temerity and summarily dismissed Rouge Croix saying that he, a King, would take no orders from a mere Earl.

Surrey was in a serious dilemma; he knew that, with the Scottish guns facing south, a direct infantry attack from Milfield Plain on the slopes of Flodden Hill would be suicidal. He also knew that supplies were low, food was short and beer was exhausted. The lack of beer was a potential disaster because beer was made from boiled water and was therefore safe to drink. Drinking stream or puddle water led to infection, dysentery and cholera and could quickly destroy an army as a fighting force.

It was now that the Bastard Heron made his appearance at the English camp. The illegitimate half-brother of the owner of Ford Castle was the local lad gone bad. He was outlawed on both sides of the Border, and wanted for the murder of the Scottish Warden of the Eastern Marches. The Bastard risked his life by just showing his face in the English camp, but he had a plan, and Surrey was willing to listen.

Taking advice from the Bastard, on the morning of September 8th, Surrey broke camp at Wooler and

The Flodden Gates At Barmoor Castle Country Park
Designed and made by local craftsman Stephen Mather

Milfield Plain From Flodden Hill
The heavy Scottish guns were arrayed near here

marched, in pouring rain, not directly towards the enemy on Flodden Hill, but east to Weetwood Bridge, and then northwards along the old Roman road, the Devil's Causeway, to Barmoor. Using this route the straggling English army was able to stay out of sight of the Scots on Flodden Hill, but the River Till on their left flank was an obstacle to be crossed before the enemy could be engaged. At Barmoor the English again made camp, Surrey and his commanders in the relative shelter of Barmoor Castle, and the ordinary soldiers under whatever cover they could find. That night English scouts must have peered into the darkness from Watchlaw in order to gain any sliver of information about the Scottish Camp over to the west on Flodden Hill. The strategic position for battle had, at a stroke, changed radically and the English suddenly held a distinct advantage. The Scots on Flodden Hill had been outflanked.

Surrey was now able to make his final plans.

Command for the Battle was to be a family affair. The Vanguard would be commanded by Edmund Howard, Surrey's younger son. The leading part of the main body of the army, including the 1000 professional soldiers brought from France, would be led by the Earl's elder son, the Lord Admiral. The Earl of Surrey himself would lead the second part of the main body. This left one more division consisting of Cheshire and Lancashire archers to be commanded by Sir Edward Stanley.

With their camp now at Barmoor, only about six

miles from the port of Berwick-upon-Tweed, the English supply lines were significantly shortened. Supplies no longer needed to be brought overland from Newcastle. The Scots had made no attempt to attack Berwick and the bridge across the Tweed was firmly in English hands. The road into Scotland was open and the route to Edinburgh was clear, leaving the Scottish capital undefended because their army was on Flodden Hill. King James could not know what Surrey's plans might be. Did he intend to wait and re-supply from Berwick? Was he going to cross the Tweed and lay waste to the Scottish Borderlands? Did he intend to march westwards and cut off the Scottish supply lines from Coldstream? Or, most devastating of all, were the English going to march north to take undefended Edinburgh, and exchange a small hill in Northumberland for the rather more valuable prize of the Scottish capital city?

The ball was now firmly in Surrey's court.

Before dawn on September 9th 1513, in pouring rain and a south-easterly gale the English army divided into three sections. The Vanguard and artillery moved northwest, almost to the River Tweed and Border to cross the River Till at Twizel Bridge. Both sections of the main body of the army crossed the Till a mile or so upstream at, or near, Castle Heaton. Stanley is thought to have left Barmoor somewhat later, and to have taken a more direct route to cross the Till probably near Etal or Ford. The Vanguard and main body crossed the Till around noon and made their final approach to Branxton from the north. By now James'

scouts must have reported the English movements and James would have realised that he must quit Flodden Hill, either to defend the north facing slopes of Branxton Hill, or perhaps to make a strategic withdrawal to the relative safety of his homeland north of the River Tweed. Whatever King's James' immediate plans may have been, his current position was untenable. His guns faced the wrong way, having been dug in to protect against an expected English attack from the south across Milfield Plain.

He had to move, and to move quickly.

We may never know whether the Scots moved to defend the high ground of Branxton Hill, or were heading for the Tweed and safety, and were intercepted during a strategic withdrawal by the approaching English. But as the two armies came in sight of each other the scene was set for the bloodiest episode in the history of these Borderlands.

Battle was inevitable.

The Battlefield

Today the Battlefield of Flodden may look very different to the landscape of five hundred years ago, but although woodland, vegetation and the way the land is used have changed substantially, the topography remains very much unaltered. In the early 1500s this would have been a treeless area of uncultivated scrub moorland, a far cry from today's ordered and contained agricultural regularity.

The Battle takes its name from Flodden Hill, a steep-sided andesite outcrop that guards the northern edge of the flat River Till flood plain of Milfield Plain. The high ground extends westwards from the summit of Flodden Hill and here is known as The King's Chair, an obvious clue to its importance as the Scottish camp. Other place names linked to the Battle are; Encampment Farm, a field called Battle Bush and a plantation called the King's Strip. About a mile to the north of the Flodden Monument at Crookham Westfield there is a standing stone that has the name, The King's Stone. It was once thought that it marked the place where King James IV fell in battle, but its relevance to Flodden is now considered to be doubtful. It is more likely to have been a "gathering stone" used in prehistory.

At the time of the Battle there were no trees on Flodden Hill, but now, when viewed from across the Till near Ford, it is marked by a distinct arrow-shaped plantation of non-native conifer trees. These trees now obscure the view of the surrounding area that the Scots would have had as they waited for the approach of Surrey and his army.

The high ground also extends northwards to a plateau and then to the ridge of Branxton Hill and Moneylaws Hill to the west. In fact, although at first sight it may not appear so, the summit of Branxton Hill is slightly higher than that of Flodden Hill. The northern slope of Branxton Hill is steep and undulating at its eastern end near Branxton village, but the slope becomes more regular and gradual further west where there now

runs a line of tall, unsightly steel electricity pylons. Here the more gentle northern slopes lead down to an area of relatively flat ground to the west of the Flodden Monument.

Near to Branxton, at the foot of the steep north facing slope of Branxton Hill lies a shallow valley, through which now runs a deep cut drainage ditch, and beyond the ditch rises a low, but significant ridge of ground. This ridge has no official name, but in this book it will be called The Howard Ridge. The Battlefield Trail interpretation boards refer to the valley as The Killing Fields and the relevance of both names will be explained on the following pages.

Branxton village has migrated westwards over the years and, with the exception of St Paul's Church, there are no buildings surviving from the time of the Battle. Branxton Tower is mentioned in ancient documents, but there is nothing today to give a clue as to its whereabouts. To the south of the Flodden Monument at the foot of Branxton Hill there are the remains of a farm steading, Branxton Steads. These buildings are ruined, and date back only to Victorian times although they were used and inhabited until the 1940s.

Another, deeper valley lies just north of the village of Branxton which even today, floods after prolonged rain and the name, the Bog Field, is an obvious indication that the ground is constantly marshy. Hidden in a modern tree plantation to the west of the Bog field is the site of Branx Brig, a small bridge across the

Flodden Hill From Ford Common
The arrowhead plantation marks the position of the Scottish camp

Pallinsburn stream over which the approaching English are said to have crossed. The possibility of this having happened is vanishingly small as the whole boggy area is likely to have been avoided by the English; but perhaps a few soldiers may have crossed the Pallinsburn here, giving rise to the local myth. Beyond the valley is yet another ridge of high ground which would have hidden all but the final approach of the English Centre Divisions from the Scots on Branxton Hill.

The Scots Vanguard and Left Centre Divisions who were positioned on the westward end of Branxton Hill would have had, through the murk and rain, a view of the Tweed Valley, and beyond that, their homeland. They would also have seen the approach of Edmund Howard's Vanguard and realised that battle was now inevitable because the English had already occupied a position that blocked their way to the River Tweed and safety.

We cannot be sure of the exact route that the Scots took in their move from Flodden to Branxton Hill. They would have moved over a broad front, but the heavy guns are likely to have been moved, as far as possible, along existing roads or tracks. Medieval roads existed running east-west between Flodden and Branxton Hills, and from the western end of Branxton Hill to a crossing point over the Tweed at Learmouth. It is worth noting that, in 500 years, the Tweed has shifted its course and Learmouth was then on the very bank of the river. On the earliest maps the only road into Branxton is shown as running from the Flodden

Hill area northwards into what is now the middle of the village. All these roads have recently shown evidence of their medieval origins.

The most striking point on the Battlefield is the granite cross of the Flodden Monument which was erected in 1910. This stands atop the small, but distinctive knoll of Stock Law, locally better known as Piper's Hill. This steep sided hill probably had little significance in the Battle itself other than the possibility that it was a useful observation point on the English battle line.

The Armies reach Branxton

It was late afternoon on September 9th when the two opposing armies finally came in sight of each other. Through the driving rain of a south-westerly gale the English saw the Scottish army arrayed along the crest of Branxton Hill, and Scotsmen almost within sight of their homeland, found their route to safety blocked by an advancing army. The English army, approaching Branxton from the north, had forced the Scots to abandon their once seemingly secure fortifications on Flodden Hill. King James had no option but to shift his heavy guns from their south facing prepared emplacements and to turn his army around and move the mile or so northwards to defend the high ground of Branxton Hill.

We will never know if King James intended to fight on Branxton Hill, or perhaps was attempting a strategic withdrawal, and was taking his prestigious and extremely valuable artillery train back across the

River Tweed to home and safety. There is opinion that Lords Home and Huntly and the Scottish Vanguard had been ordered to move to guard the crossing point of the Tweed near Coldstream and, if this was the case, it is strong evidence that the defence of his homeland was now James' primary objective.

Whatever James' intention might have been, his forces were now confronted by an English army moving into position between Branxton Hill and Scotland. Possibilities for James were now limited, to fight or to run; and to run was not an option for a King at the head of his army. Even so, James' confidence would have been high. He held the high ground and he had the most modern military hardware. His army was rested and well provisioned, and they outnumbered the English who now hurriedly moved into battle formation on the lower ground to the north of Branxton Hill.

What James could not see were two additional English divisions. Ahead the light cavalry of Lord Dacre's Borderers who were hidden behind the English Centre in a shallow valley just to the north of the village of Branxton, and still distant were Sir Edward Stanley's archers. Stanley had left Barmoor later than the rest of the English army and had taken a different route to Branxton, crossing the River Till near Ford, but was still some distance from the impending Battle.

Stanley's late arrival on the field of battle was to prove to be critical to the outcome of Flodden.

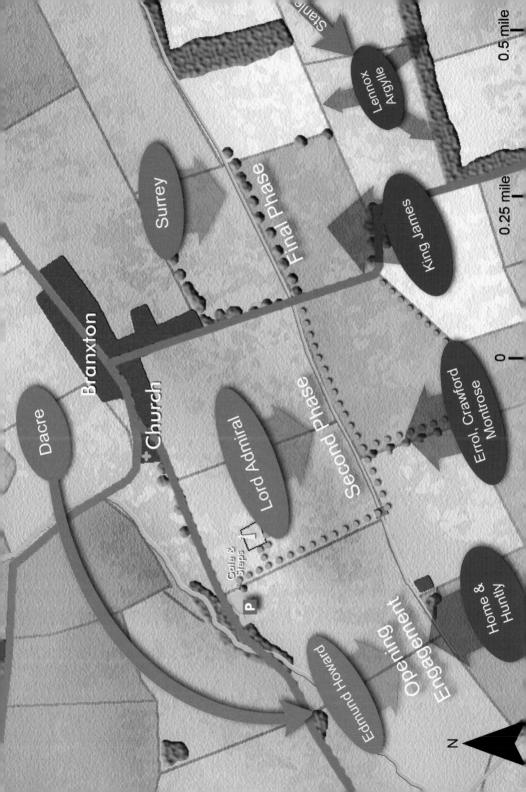

Dacre

Branxton

Surrey

Church

Lennox
Argylle

Stanle

Final Phase

King James

Lord Admiral

Second Phase

Gate &
Steps

P

Errol, Crawford
Montrose

Edmund Howard

Opening
Engagement

Home &
Huntly

N

0   0.25 mile   0.5 mile

The Battle

"The history of a battle is not unlike the history of a ball. Some individuals may recollect all the little events of which the great result is the battle won or lost, but no individual can recollect the order in which, or the exact moment at which, they occurred, which makes all the difference as to their value or importance."

Arthur Wellesley, 1st Duke of Wellington

The Opening Engagement

From Branxton Hill the Scots could see, on their left, the English Vanguard commanded by Edmund Howard. Directly ahead, the largest English Division, the Centre commanded by The Lord Admiral, and to their right, the Earl of Surrey. The English Vanguard consisting of some 3000 troops was first into position, moving onto the flat ground about a half mile to the west of Branxton. They faced the much larger division of Lords Home and Huntly on the Scottish left.

Battle opened with an artillery exchange. It is not certain exactly where this took place, but it is likely that the prized and prestigious Scottish guns were being moved to safety with Home and Huntly's leading Division. On the route to Battle, the English artillery had crossed over Twizel Bridge with the Vanguard, and it is probable that it remained with Edmund Howard on the final approach. This makes the fields to the west of the Flodden Monument the most likely location for the artillery exchange. There is evidence to support this theory as small composite round shot has been found on the flat ground to the west of the Flodden monument.

Being light, easy to move, aim and reload, the English guns soon had the better of this early artillery exchange. Many accounts speak of the English destroying the Scottish guns and gunners, but this may not strictly be the case.

The main, and much prized Scottish guns were modern, but heavy muzzle loaders and they fired a large iron ball of up to 60 lbs weight. The recoil was substantial. This necessitated the guns to be re-sited and aimed after each shot and, after the hurried move from Flodden Hill, there had been no time to dig them into workable and defensive emplacements. The heavy bronze guns also overheated rapidly and this also severely limited their rate of fire. On the heights of Branxton Hill there was no water available for cooling red-hot gun barrels.

The lighter English field guns had the advantage of easy manoeuvrability and, being breech-loaders, were quick and easy to reload and fire. Although firing only a small composite iron cored lead ball, not much bigger than a golf ball, the English guns were of high muzzle velocity, and shot in a flat trajectory. Shooting uphill was an advantage as their target was the large massed ranks of Scottish pikemen and the ball could split, fracture and cut a swathe through these tightly packed ranks, and each shot caused many casualties. In contrast the heavy Scottish cannon balls were

60

hurled downhill in a parabolic trajectory at relatively low speed and would crash and disappear into the soft ground causing few or no casualties because they did not bounce and cause havoc and confusion as did the English round shot.

It may well have been that the slow rate of fire of the Scottish guns gave the impression that they had been knocked out by English fire. Whatever the case, the noise of the artillery was something new and utterly terrifying for the soldiers on both sides, and the Scots may well have been galled into premature movement by this unprecedented experience of death from a distance.

The first troops to move into action in the Battle of Flodden were the Scottish left flank when the pikes of Home and Huntly started down the gentle and regular slope at the western end of Branxton Hill to engage Edmund Howard's English Vanguard.

It is possible that this Division had been sent by James with orders to secure the crossing over the Tweed, but were caught on Branxton Hill by the approaching English Vanguard. If this was the case then the rest of the Scottish army would have followed, and James' intention would certainly have been to beat a strategic retreat to the home country on the safer northern bank of the Tweed. James' notion of chivalry would have allowed this as he had agreed to wait and join battle by noon on the 9th, and it was by now late afternoon and there were only a few hours of daylight left.

Perhaps the Scots were caught on Branxton Hill during an attempted retreat, but had they moved a couple of hours earlier or later then the outcome of the Battle of Flodden would have been very different.

The Scottish Left under Home and Huntly made their move as Edmund Howard's Vanguard reached the field of combat and hurriedly moved into fighting formation. Their artillery barrage had ceased, but the English guns continued to fire and cause Scottish casualties as the Scots closed for battle. The pikes were able to keep close formation on this easy descent and engaged Howard on the flat land a few hundred yards to the west of the Flodden Monument. Recently two small cannon balls have been found in these fields and a bone pit is marked on an early OS map providing good evidence that action took place around here.

Home and Huntly's Division greatly outnumbered Edmund Howard's Vanguard and quickly gained the upper hand. Unable to withstand the Scottish pikes, many English ran from the field, and Howard was three times struck to the ground. Seeing the imminent danger of a rout, Howard tore the Agnus Dei medallion from around his neck and sent it via his Herald to the Earl of Surrey with an urgent and desperate plea for immediate reinforcements. The English deserters who were running from the field were most probably a part of Stanley's contingent who, at Barmoor, had been placed in the Vanguard under Edmund Howard's command. They considered that their loyalties were to Stanley and they had expected to fight under the Stanley banner. They might well have been persuaded

The Opening Engagement
Took place on the flat ground west of the monument

to fight alongside their neighbours for their local Lord, but not among strangers and for a commander they did not know, or trust. First the noise and terror of an artillery barrage and then the overwhelming onslaught of Scottish pikes convinced them that this was more than duty demanded.

Surrey quickly saw the impending peril and instantly ordered the light cavalry of Dacre and his Borderers to ride to his son's aid.

Unseen by the Scottish Centre Division on Branxton Hill, Dacre's horses galloped through the valley to the north of Branxton and arrived just in time to save the life of Edmund Howard and to prevent a complete rout of the English Vanguard.

This intervention saved the day for England.

The Scottish Left, unable to complete the destruction of the English Vanguard, were themselves now in disarray and the pike schiltrons had lost their essential tight formation. The pikes should have been able to provide an excellent defence against Dacre's light cavalry, but it must be remembered that the Scots had little time to train in the use of pikes, and this might have been beyond their capabilities.

The Scottish Vanguard was unable to move into a flanking attack on the right of the English Centre Division.

For whatever reason, Home and Huntly now left the

field and took no further part in the Battle of Flodden. Home declared that they "had done their bit and the rest should do likewise".

For this action, or lack of, Home's reputation was dashed and he was later executed for his part in the struggle for power in the years of the Regency during the infancy of James V.

The Second Phase of Battle

The optimistic perception of the course of the Battle from the position of the Scottish Centre on Branxton Hill was somewhat premature. In the early stages things appeared to be going well and soldiers could be seen running from the field. In the rain and murky conditions it would have been difficult to distinguish between fleeing English, and rampaging Scots charging towards the undefended flank of the English Centre Division. Either situation would have fitted well with the Scottish battle plan.

The Scottish Centre Division commanded by the Earls Lennox, Crawford and Montrose began their move down Branxton Hill to engage the largest English contingent under the command of Surrey's elder son, the Lord Admiral. The English were positioned on the Howard Ridge to the south of Branxton village between the Flodden Monument and the road to Branxton Hill. At this stage the Scots were unaware of Dacre's light cavalry as they galloped unseen through the valley to the north of Branxton on their vital rescue mission.

The Scots also had another problem, they did not appreciate the steepness of the slope of Branxton Hill at this point and they had no awareness of the ground conditions at the foot of Branxton Hill a combination of circumstances that was to prove to be disastrous.

The close packed ranks of pikes made their way down the slope in silence, but as the front ranks reached the shallow valley between Branxton Hill and the Howard Ridge the ground conditions worsened. The geology here gives rise to increasing amounts of surface water towards the lower edge of the slope and ranks of tramping feet soon churned up the ground. Progress was slow and then, at the base of the slope, halted as the pikemen found themselves knee deep in cloying mud and the ground gave way and began to resemble quicksand. The ranks behind still pressed on and those at the front faltered, stumbled and many fell to be tramped and suffocated in the mire.

An ordered advance rapidly became chaotic.

The first assault from the English came from the archers, but the Scots were well armoured and the wet weather had slackened the English bowstrings, and the feared English longbow did not live up to its formidable reputation. The archers would however have had a very significant effect on the advancing Scots. Placed on the flanks of the English Centre Division, arrow storms of thousands of deadly missiles would have funnelled the Scots into a narrower attacking front and so increased the compaction, the confusion, the chaos and the killing.

The Hidden Valley North of Branxton
Dacre galloped through here to rescue the English Vanguard

With the Scots advance in disarray, and the English on the Howard Ridge now holding the higher ground, it was time for the English billhook to start its bloody work. The Scots struggled through the boggy morass in ones and twos rather than a strong, close-packed line of fearsome spears. Their unwieldy 18 ft pikes were now of little use, and more of an encumbrance than a useable weapon. Further impeded by dead and dying bodies the Scots fell easy prey to the shorter, but more manoeuvrable and versatile billhook, which now had a length advantage over the Scots' secondary hand-held weapons of sword, dagger and axe.

In hand to hand close quarter fighting the slaughter was dreadful. The commanders, Earls Lennox, Crawford and Montrose died in battle alongside their countrymen. No help came from Home and Huntly whose Division had left the field rather than regroup and attempt to roll down the English flank. Had they departed to secure the crossing over the Tweed?

Within the space of a few yards the course of the Battle of Flodden had changed.

The Final Phase of Battle

After the seeming success of the first encounter the tables had been turned. The Scots of King James' Division on the right flank, still on the heights of Branxton Hill, could see the carnage taking place in the valley below. James' one chance of victory now was to kill or capture the English Commander, the Earl of Surrey. This Scottish Division was superior in numbers to that of the Earl of Surrey and held the high ground, but Surrey showed no signs of advancing up the slope of Branxton Hill.

It was now that King James IV of Scotland made his crucial decision.

Rather than stay and command the battle from a vantage point on Branxton Hill, James considered that chivalry demanded that he fought in combat alongside his men. He now committed his Division to the fray, and descended Branxton Hill close to where the road runs into the village. Here the slope of Branxton Hill is steep, and it is also undulating. Keeping the ranks of pikes in a straight line would have been difficult if not impossible and the same boggy morass at the base of Branxton Hill awaited them. James was determined to reach the Earl of Surrey. He fought through the mêlée towards the Earl's banner, but Surrey was well protected by his retinue of bodyguards.

Surrey's Division was by now being reinforced by the Lord Admiral's Centre and James was in a desperate and deadly situation. The cutting, thrusting, hacking billhooks were again proving to be more effective weapons than the long unwieldy pikes as the English defended their elevated position on the eastern end of the Howard Ridge.

In deciding to fight with his soldiers rather than command from a strategic point on Branxton Hill, James had made a disastrous error. In the King's eyes chivalry may well have demanded this course of action,

The Killing Fields At The Base Of Branxton Hill
With the Howard Ridge beyond

but militarily it was a fundamental mistake. James immediately lost control of the overall management of the battle and in the mêlée he became an accessible target for any English soldier.

But, there was one uncommitted Scottish Division remaining on Branxton Hill which might still make a difference and perhaps save the day. This was the 5000 to 6000 free-ranging, hard-fighting Highlanders under the command of Earls Lennox and Argyll. They were armed not with pikes, but with the more traditional claymore and battle-axe. Seeing their King in mortal peril the Highlanders started down Branxton Hill to his rescue. It was now that Sir Edward Stanley appeared on the scene with archers drawn from his Lancashire and Cheshire estates.

Stanley had left Barmoor after the main body and had taken a different route to the Battle. Early documents show that he came via Sandyford, Crookham Dene and Pace Hill, to arrive along the top of Branxton Hill just as the Highlanders made ready to move down the slope. The Highlanders although armed with claymores and battle axes had little in the way of body armour. In contrast to the much better protected pike men the Highlanders had little defence against the deadly long range English arrows. In what was probably the last devastating use of the English longbow in battle, the men of this last Scottish Division were caught in a broadside attack. Volleys of arrows from Stanley's archers tore into the Highlanders and, suffering heavy casualties, they were scattered and unable to retain their order as a fighting unit.

The confusion and disruption of this late attack prevented any chance of the King's retreat from the final mêlée of the Battle of Flodden. Surrey was now being reinforced by troops from the victorious Lord Admiral's Division, and James' fate was sealed.

As daylight began to fail on this wet and stormy September day King James IV of Scotland fell. Struck by arrows and hacked by billhook, he became the last monarch to die in battle in the British Isles. With their King, many members of the Scottish noble families also died.

Casualties among the common soldiers were horrific; some 10,000 Scots and 4,000 English within the space of four hours and along a battlefront of less than a mile; figures that compare to some of the worst episodes on the Somme in the First World War. Scotland suffered greatly, losing her King, 9 Earls, 14 Lords of Parliament, and 79 gentry. It is said that no Scottish noble family escaped loss.

English casualties were lighter, but they did not lose leaders, members of the nobility or experienced military commanders. It was no walkover. Four thousand dead from the conscripted levies from towns and villages of the northern counties left a mark for a generation.

> *"Believe me, nothing except a battle lost can be half so melancholy as a battle won".*
>
> *Arthur Wellesley, 1st Duke of Wellington*

The main factors in the outcome of the Battle of Flodden are still debatable, but there is little doubt that, on the day, the English guns were better suited to the job. The pikes were successful in the early stages, but hampered by the boggy ground, proved useless when most needed. Against the pike the billhook was a simple, effective and brutal weapon.

The longbow was at the end of its military usefulness and had mixed results. Against well-armoured soldiers it was of little use, especially as the wet weather reduced its effectiveness by allowing the bowstring to stretch and therefore weaken, but against lightly or non armoured targets it was still a devastating weapon.

There can be little doubt that Surrey was a skilled and hardened military campaigner and that he brought to Flodden all his experience of previous conflict, including being on the losing side at Bosworth.

James IV was Scotland's Renaissance King, patron of the arts, builder of a modern navy, and eager to encompass the latest tactics and equipment of warfare. A chivalrous leader, he was keen to add success in battle to his accomplishments, but he has little claim to being a good General or military leader. On the 9th of September 1513 James IV of Scotland was outmanoeuvred by a wily, 71 year old survivor of Bosworth and other military conflicts.

Surrey took risks, but he also took advice from those with local knowledge. He did not do as expected, and followed his own battle plan, rather than that of King James. Perhaps Surrey's real genius was, at the last minute, to change his attacking manoeuvre into a position of defence. By waiting on the Howard Ridge and letting the Scots advance, Surrey gained a massive advantage. Either Surrey knew about the ground conditions at the foot of Branxton Hill, or else he had luck on his side. And luck is the most important quality for any General.

One factor that has changed little over the past 500 years is the topography of the battlefield. The hills remain the same even though the vegetation has changed. In spite of there now being a deep drainage ditch, after wet weather the valley at the base of Branxton Hill still floods and the boggy ground reappears. The changing perspective of the English held ridge still amazes as you walk down the steep north facing slopes of Branxton Hill. Valleys continue to hide from view as you move through the place where the Scots waited for battle to begin.

It is perhaps only on the Battlefield itself that you can fully appreciate how in 1513 the landscape and the topography of this quiet corner of northern England was the real key to success or despair on that fateful September day.

Flodden was a battle that the Scots should have expected to win. They had the larger army, more modern kit and they held a strongly fortified defensive position on Flodden Hill. James made the mistake of assuming that his opponent would do as expected

The Killling Fields Valley
after prolonged winter rain

and attack Flodden's southern slopes. Perhaps James had thought that Surrey, with whom he was well acquainted, would be satisfied with nominal show of force and exchange of a few cannon balls and then both sides would retire and claim that honour had been satisfied.

Surrey however was made of sterner stuff. The Howard family had, over the preceding years, seen success and failure, influence and rejection, a Dukedom won and lost. Surrey had worked his way from imprisonment in the Tower of London to being a trusted advisor to the English Crown and now, at the age of seventy, he realised that this was his last chance for greatness.

He knew that a decisive victory here would secure the Howard family's influence and fortune.

The Aftermath

Few would argue that the Battle of Flodden was a disaster for Scotland. James IV was Scotland's renaissance King and his loss alone would have been a tragedy, but to lose such a great part of the ruling hierarchy, and to deprive so many families of their breadwinners was a catastrophe that would affect Scotland for decades. Add to this the passing of the throne to the infant James V and the resulting squabbles of a long lasting Regency, and Scotland's influence was severely diminished.

Although Flodden has marked Scotland's collective psyche to this day, it was not a triumph for England.

English casualties, though not as severe as Scotland's, were significant and many towns and villages south of the Border also felt the pain of their loss.   But Flodden was not the military victory that Henry VIII desperately wanted.   True, he had his minor triumph in France by winning The Battle of the Spurs, but although the State Papers of the time make much of it, this was little more than a skirmish and had no real military significance.   The victory at Flodden belonged to Henry's Regent, his wife, Catherine of Aragon.   This must have exasperated and frustrated the proud young King, and their subsequent estrangement and divorce ensured that, south of the Border, the importance of Flodden was officially diminished.

The real winners at Flodden were the Earl of Surrey and the Howard family.   The following year Thomas Howard, the Earl of Surrey was reinstated to the Dukedom of Norfolk and Howard influence was again on the ascendency.   During a roller coaster ride back to a position as one of the most important and manipulative families in England, the Howards provided, with varying degrees of success, wives and mistresses to Henry VIII.   Anne Boleyn and Catherine Howard, both closely related to Surrey, (now Norfolk) became Henry's second and fifth wife, with both sharing a similar fate on the executioner's block.

The Lord Admiral succeeded to the Earldom of Surrey and later, on his father's death, became the third Duke of Norfolk. In the turbulent and uncertain times towards the end of Henry's reign he was arraigned for treason, stripped of the Dukedom and, in the Howard tradition, sentenced to the block. But incredibly the Howard luck held, and the night before the execution, Henry VIII died and the third Duke was reinstated and lived for a further seven years.

Henry VIII was succeeded to the throne of England by three of his offspring: Edward VI, son of Jane Seymour; Mary I, daughter of Catherine of Aragon; and Elizabeth I, daughter of Anne Boleyn. But none of these produced further issue and the Tudor dynasty ended.

Ninety years after the Battle of Flodden, following the death of Elizabeth I, the succession to the Throne of England moved sideways to the line of Henry's sister Margaret and her husband James IV of Scotland. In 1603, King James VI of Scotland crossed the River Tweed at Berwick on his way to London to become also King James I of England, thus uniting the two once warring nations under the one monarch.

Howard Family Twig

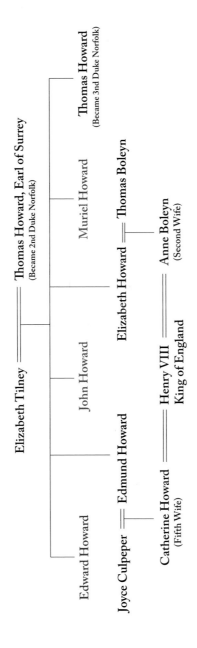

Fig 1

81

Tudor Family Twig

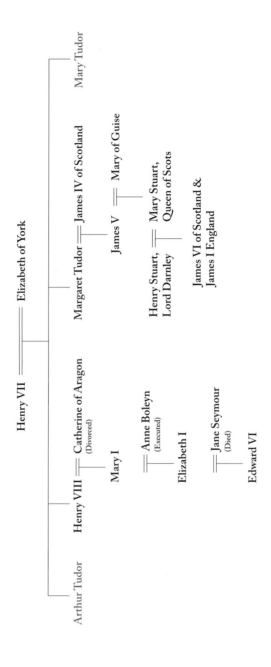

Arthur Tudor

Henry VII ═══ Elizabeth of York

Henry VIII ═══ Catherine of Aragon
(Divorced)

Mary I

═══ Anne Boleyn
(Executed)

Elizabeth I

═══ Jane Seymour
(Died)

Edward VI

Margaret Tudor ═══ James IV of Scotland

James V ═══ Mary of Guise

Henry Stuart, ═══ Mary Stuart,
Lord Darnley   Queen of Scots

James VI of Scotland &
James I England

Mary Tudor

Fig 2

The Flodden Battlefield Trail

The View from the English Battle Lines

The Flodden Monument

On the height of the hill known as Stock Law or Piper's Hill, a few hundred yards to the west of Branxton village, stands the Flodden Monument, a stark granite cross and perhaps one of the most iconic battlefield memorials of all. It is dedicated

TO THE BRAVE OF BOTH NATIONS

The Monument overlooks Flodden Field from a vantage point that may well have been used 500 years ago by the Lord Admiral in the English Centre as he watched the ebb and flow, and the changing fortunes of battle. Today this is still a good place to view the Battlefield and work out how the two armies might have manoeuvred, advanced and engaged in mortal combat. Here, the first of a series of interpretation boards, *Battle Lines are Drawn*, explains what may have happened, and why events unfolded as they did.

The Battlefield Trail

From the car park which is to be found in "Dickie's Den", a small wooded area about 400 yards to the west of St Paul's Church, Branxton, make your way up the steps to the Monument switch your mind back five hundred years and imagine that you are a soldier of the Lord Admiral's Centre Division. The weather is foul, a south easterly gale and driving rain into your

Battlefield Trail
Interpretation Board
Permissive Footpath
Public Right of Way

0.5 m

0.25 mile

Surrey Wood

King
James
Wood

Boggy Ground

Hidden Valley

Branxton

Church

Howard Ridge

Boggy Ground

Steep Slope

Flodden
Monument

Line of
Oak Tree

Ruined Farm

P

N

face and you are dog tired after an eleven mile march from last night's camp at Barmoor. You have marched, with full kit, almost to the River Tweed and Scottish Border, waded across the River Till and then come to the field of battle from the north. Now, as you stand at the top of Piper's Hill look southwards towards Branxton Hill. You can see the Scottish army arrayed in three divisions. You cannot see a fourth division, the Highlanders of Lennox and Argyll who are positioned to the rear of King James' Right Wing which is close to the road running down Branxton Hill into Branxton village.

You can see and hear the flash and crash of cannon. You can see clouds of dense smoke and you can smell and even feel the acrid taste of gunpowder in your mouth. You sense the thud and thump of heavy cannon balls as they fall around you. The noise, the sight, the smell, the fear; neither you nor your fellow soldiers have ever experienced such appalling conditions.

It is as if the very gates of Hell have opened around you.

The heavy Scottish guns are firing from close to the crest of Branxton Hill, but they are slow to reload and fire and have to be repositioned after every shot. The large cannon balls that drop nearby come in at a steep angle and squelch into the soft ground. There are casualties, but these are few, as the balls do not bounce, and do not cause multiple deaths and injury.

By contrast, the English guns although old, are

Map 3 - The Battlefield Trail   85

lightweight and easy to move and aim. These light field guns are brought up to the firing line and advance with the soldiers, firing and moving to gain the best position to cause the most damage to the enemy and to raise the morale of your own troops.

Teams of gunners work to recharge the removable breach pieces and the rate of fire is many times faster then that of the Scottish guns. The accuracy of the English guns is also much better. They are small, but powerful. The muzzle velocity of the round shot is very high. They shoot in a low, flat trajectory and shooting uphill is easier and more effective because the ground at the target is parallel to the flight of the round shot.

The small, iron cored lead balls are cutting swathes through the closely packed Scottish ranks. They tear into flesh, bone and armour, and shatter into small fragmented pieces. This is "death from a distance". The Scots, rather than stand and take casualties, are forced into action.

To your right, about two fields away, on the flat ground Edmund Howard's Vanguard is moving forward to counter the much larger Scottish force of Home and Huntly as the close-packed ranks of pikes make their way in good order down the gentle slopes of Branxton Hill. This would have been close to where the line of pylons now stands. There is evidence of conflict in the fields west of the monument; a bone pit is marked on an O.S. early map and two small iron and lead composite round shot, barely larger than a golf ball, were recently found.

Branxton Hill From The Flodden Monument
Looking towards the position of the Scottish Centre

The Scottish pikes soon have the advantage and begin to overcome Edmund Howard's smaller Division. Some English solders do not stand their ground and take fright and start to flee the battlefield. Howard is wounded, and three times struck to the ground. He realises the severity of his situation and how close he is to failure and a rout of his Division. Howard knows that should this happen, the Scots will then be able to roll down the right flank of the English Centre, just where you now stand. The Scottish Centre Division directly to your front will then move forward from the heights of Branxton Hill and you will be caught by overwhelming enemy numbers in a deadly and inescapable pincer move.

Defeat and disaster are staring you in the face.

In desperation Howard tears his Agnus Dei medallion from his neck, hands it to a Herald and sends it as proof of identity to his father with a frantic plea for reinforcements before all is lost.

The English Commander, the Earl of Surrey, wastes no time and directs Lord Dacre's Borderers, with 1500 or so light cavalry to ride to the rescue of his beleaguered son and the English Vanguard. This Dacre does, galloping with all speed through the valley behind you and, unseen by the Scots on Branxton Hill, brings the vital reinforcements which steady the resolve of the English Vanguard and saves the life of Edmund Howard. The Scottish pikes have by now lost their tight formation in the encounter and the arrival of fresh fighting troops is sufficient to scatter the

The Start of The Battlefield Trail
The trail starts near the monument and goes over the Howard Ridge towards Branxton Hill

The Flat Ground To The West of The Flodden Monument
where the opening action of the battle took place

disordered Scots and prevent their further advance.

For whatever reason, perhaps to re-group and re-form, or to go and secure and guard the crossing point over the river Tweed, this Scottish contingent now leaves the field of battle and Home and Huntly take no further part in the Battle of Flodden.

For now, the day has been saved for England.

It is now that the Lord Admiral's Centre Division must join battle.

Take the path at the western edge of the Monument field southwards to the Howard Ridge and towards Branxton Hill.

The Howard Ridge and the Valley

As you walk along this path you are walking in the steps of the Lord Admiral's soldiers as they moved forward to join battle with the Scots who now are descending the slope of Branxton Hill. You are aware of the close-run fight that has been raging a few hundred yards to your right, and you are in dread of the fate that awaits you as the pikes of the Scottish Centre under the command of Lords Errol, Crawford and Montrose steadily, inevitably, come at you from the heights of Branxton Hill. You know you must go forward because the Lord Admiral has 1000 professional soldiers with him and any attempt to run will be dealt with in a quick and simple manner.

Your only chance of survival is to go forward.

The Northern Slope of Branxton Hill
seen from the Howard Ridge

As you move towards the enemy you reach the Howard Ridge and you can see that before you there is a valley. It is not deep, but the slope on your side is steep, and the Scots must climb this before they can use their pikes. You hold your nerve and yard by yard you begin to understand that the topography and ground is in your favour.

As you make your way forward towards the enemy you reach a point where you realise that the ground in the valley is not firm. It is a wet and boggy morass. The Scots must get through this and you, on the Howard Ridge, now hold the dry, firm, higher ground.

Your confidence increases.

Then you see that the packed ranks of the pike schiltrons are faltering. The Scots below you are up to their knees in cloying mud. The front ranks of pikes are slowed, and then halted, but the rearward ranks still push forward. They crush the stumbling leading pikemen into the mire. Your commander calls in the archers and thousands of arrows from English longbows tear into the Scots from both flanks of your advancing Division. The deadly missiles funnel the floundering Scots into an ever narrowing front. The crush and confusion increases as the faltering Scots now find their progress further impeded by the dead and dying bodies of their countrymen.

But the arrows are not stopping the Scots. The wet weather has slackened bow strings and reduced the longbows' killing force, and the front ranks of pikemen are well armoured. Many arrows bounce away causing little or no harm. But the momentum, the forward movement of the pikes has been lost. There is no longer the solid phalanx of deadly 18 ft long spears moving forward with relentless progress; instead the enemy is coming at you in ones, twos, or in small groups. The Scots struggle through the mud, over their own dead, and clamber up the steep slope towards you. Their pikes have become a hindrance and are useless in small numbers. They are dropped, or thrown away.

The English archers have not won the Battle, but they have done their job.

They have created a killing zone.

You feel that you now have a chance of survival.

It is now that your 8 ft billhook outreaches the Scottish hand weapons of sword and battle axe and can be used, jabbing, cutting, hacking, thrusting, to its bloody advantage.

The conflict becomes murderous.

No prisoners are taken.

Blood soaks the ground.

In the valley, just by the small bridge that crosses the modern drainage ditch there is an interpretation board, *Armed for the Fight* that describes the different weapons used by the two armies.

The path crosses the small bridge over the modern drainage ditch and turns left along the field and continues along the valley.

It is along here that the Scottish Centre was halted and arrows from English longbows rained down on faltering Scottish pike men. To your left you can see that the English Centre of the Lord Admiral now holds the high ground. The Howard Ridge is now an obstacle that, even if the Scots are able to struggle through this muddy valley, now blocks further progress. It is here that the billhook started its bloody work. It is here that the Scottish commanders, Lords Errol, Crawford and Montrose died in battle alongside so many of their countrymen.

It was here that the tide of the Battle changed.

The path continues along the valley to the field gate where, alongside the line of oak trees, it climbs the slope of Branxton Hill.

Should you wish to avoid the climb, continue along the valley to the road where there is an interpretation board entitled *The Killing Fields*.

Turn right and make your way up the side of Branxton Hill (there are a couple of benches on this section of the Trail should you need a breather). You can imagine what it would have been like for the English, if they had taken the initiative and attacked first rather than hold their ground on the Howard Ridge. It would have been suicidal for them to have struggled through the

The Valley between Branxton and The Howard Ridge
This was the boggy ground that halted the Scottish Pikes

boggy ground and, carrying weapons and with the weight of armour, then make this climb into gunfire and a defensive line of pikes.

The steep slope also causes problems on the way down if you are confined in the tightly packed ranks of a pike schiltron, carrying an unwieldy 18 ft long pike.

As you make the climb stop and look around and notice how your perception of the Howard Ridge alters as you reach the top of the Battlefield Trail.

The higher you go the less of an impediment it looks, until at the top of the line of oaks the Howard Ridge has lost all semblance of being a hindrance to progress.

You can now see the Battlefield from the perspective of the Scottish soldiers.

The View from the Scottish Battle Lines

Branxton Hill

At the top of the line of oaks you can turn and view the Battlefield from the Scottish lines.

On the 9th of September 1513 the south-westerly gale and driving rain was behind you and was blowing into the faces of the oncoming English. Visibility was poor and the approaching armies did not see each other until they were almost within range of cannon shot.

But on a fine day, with the winding, glistening strand of the river marking the Border between England and

The Battlefield Trail From Branxton Hill
Looking from the position of the Scottish Centre

Scotland, the view of the Tweed Valley is spectacular. Anything that you see beyond the immediate horizon is Scotland, and for the Scottish soldiers as they lined up for battle this meant home and safety.

It is worth noting that here, where you now stand, marks the position of the Scottish Centre Division, and you cannot see the start positions of the Scottish Right or Left Divisions. Communications were difficult and erratic. You cannot see the pikes of Home and Huntly as they move down the slope at the western end of Branxton hill. They are not visible from here until they engage Edmund Howard's Vanguard on the flat ground to the west of the Monument. From here the conflict appeared, at first, to be going well for the Scots and this perhaps explains the timing of this second phase of the Battle.

From here you can see the lines of approach of the English contingents; to your left, along the line of pylons, Edmund Howard with the English Vanguard; ahead in the Monument field, the Lord Admiral's Centre Division; and to your right, close to where you can see the large red-brick Pallinsburn House, the Earl of Surrey's Division.

The interpretation board here entitled *Ready for the Fray* is, we freely admit, in the wrong place. It depicts the start of the descent to battle of Hume and Huntly's Division, and the board was intended to be placed on the roadside further to the west. However, problems with officialdom and insurance liabilities dictated that we place the board on the footpath rather than

The Howard Ridge
seen from Branxton Hill

the roadside, and this is the furthest west and nearest practicable location to the action depicted.

Now take the path eastwards along Branxton Hill. Flodden Hill is about a mile to the south east and James' heavy guns had that morning been hauled from their prepared emplacements and reached this position as the English army came into sight. Each heavy gun was hauled by a team of thirty or more oxen, and even more beasts and carts were needed to bring supplies of powder, shot, spares and feedstuffs for draft animals. Moving and repositioning the artillery for firing was not a quick or easy task.

An interpretation board, *Outflanked*, at the highest point of the Battlefield Trail depicts moving one of the heavy Scottish guns.

A little way further along the Trail, a board entitled, *Let Battle Commence*, depicts the Scottish Centre Division as they start their move down Branxton Hill. At this stage the Battle appears to be going well for the Scots. In spite of taking early casualties in the opening barrage from the English guns, Home and Huntly Division has attacked and the English Vanguard has no defence against Scottish pikes. English soldiers are running from the field.

Perhaps the perception from here was even more optimistic. In the murky conditions it may have appeared that it is Scottish soldiers breaking from the encounter and running towards the English Centre. Now is the time for the Scottish Centre to advance and capture this largest of the English Divisions in a pincer move.

If this is successful, the day is won for Scotland.

From here the Howard Ridge does not appear to be much of an obstacle. From here it does not seem very high, and the slope that must be climbed does not look to be very steep. You are also unaware of the ground conditions that you will meet as you reach the valley floor.

Close to the road an interpretation board, *The Scottish Battle Line*, explains the final phase of the Battle of Flodden.

As you come towards the road you approach King James' position at the start of the Battle. The Battle has been raging now for about three hours and from here you can see that the Centre is in trouble. Now the only chance for James to save the day for Scotland is to reach the English commander, the Earl of Surrey and either kill him or take him captive. It is now that James makes his fatal decision. He believes that chivalry demands that, rather than command from the relative safety of Branxton Hill, he should share the risk of battle and fight alongside his soldiers.

Leading from the front King James moves down Branxton Hill in search of his target, the Earl of Surrey.

From here you can see the steepness of the slope of

Branxton Hill and the uneven contours of the field across the road. This is not good pike country and keeping the ranks of pikes in line and tight formation is difficult, and near impossible for soldiers with little training. Again, the Scots are unaware of the boggy ground conditions at the foot of Branxton Hill, and a similar fate to that of their countrymen of the Centre Division awaits them.

King James IV has made a fatal decision.

The original Battlefield Trail now leads along the road down Branxton Hill to the valley and *The Killing Fields* interpretation board.

Here you have two options:

1. Take the road down Branxton Hill to the Killing Fields interpretation board, and return to the Monument car park either through the valley, or through Branxton village.

2. Continue 100 yards eastwards along the road on Branxton Hill to the gate in the wooded area on the left hand side. This path is described in the section Stanley's Late Arrival (see page 109).

The Killing Fields

As you walk down Branxton Hill you can imagine how your heavy, 18 ft long pike would tend to tip you forward and pull you down the slope, and how the ranks behind you would push. The gradient steepens near the valley bottom, and if you look to your right you can see how the ground undulates. Keeping straight ranks and the essential tight formation would have been almost impossible. As you reach the foot of Branxton Hill your whole aspect of the Battlefield changes within the space of a few yards. You no longer hold the high ground, your feet are becoming engulfed in cloying mud, and you now have to look upwards to see English archers and billmen on the Howard Ridge.

You are in the final mêlée of the Battle of Flodden.

It is here that the most desperate hand to hand fighting reached its bloody climax, and the worst of the slaughter took place.

Did the English know about the ground conditions? Did the Bastard Heron's local knowledge extend to such details, and had he made the Earl of Surrey aware of the problem?

From the valley floor the height and steepness of the Howard Ridge becomes obvious. From here it becomes an obstacle for the attacking Scots. You can see that holding this high ground is a distinct military advantage. By not moving from here the English turn their attacking manoeuvre into a strong defensive position.

When you reach the interpretation board The Killing Fields, look across the road towards the western end of Branxton Hill. You can see the uneven and undulating slope, and imagine how difficult it would be to bring pike schiltrons down here and still keep

Branxton Hill from the Howard Ridge
Looking towards the starting position of King James' division

The Final Melee
King James IV of Scotland was killed in battle near here.

a tight, fighting formation. From the valley you can also see how, within a few yards, the Scottish situation changes drastically. As they descended Branxton Hill, the Scottish pikes lost the height advantage, and then, while struggling through knee deep mud, were confronted by the steep slope of the Howard Ridge and English archers and billmen.

King James is now fighting for his very life. He is a target for every English archer and billman.

He pushes and hacks his way forward, and desperately tries to find a way towards Surrey. But the English Commander is well protected by his personal retinue of bodyguards. Progress is hard, vicious and slow. James' mission becomes even more difficult because reinforcements are arriving from the Lord Admiral's Division.

The King's situation is desperate.

Unknown to James, his last chance of salvation has now been lost. His last uncommitted Division, the Highlanders under the command of Lennox and Argyll do not appear.

They will not appear.

This last hope has been lost. The arrival of Stanley and his archers along the crest of Branxton Hill has caught the Highlanders in a shattering flank attack. In what was probably the last effective use of the longbow in battle, the lightly armoured Highlanders have been

**"The World's Smallest
Visitor Centre"**

**The Display in "The Visitor
Centre"**

stopped and scattered by arrow storms against which they have no defence. Their casualties are heavy and they are unable to come to the rescue of their King.

We believe that in this valley, close to the road, King James IV of Scotland fell in the final mêlée of the Battle of Flodden.

With the death of their King, for Scotland, the Battle was lost. James became the last monarch to die in battle in the British Isles.

In the failing light of September 9th 1513 the scale of Scotland's disaster became apparent. Scotland lost not only her King, but also Earls, 14 Lords of Parliament, and 79 gentry. It is said that no Scottish noble family escaped loss.

Losses among the common soldiers were horrific and compared with some of the catastrophic episodes on the Somme. Within the space of a few hours, and along a battle front of just over a mile some 10,000 Scots and 4,000 English died in hand to hand fighting. The scale of the losses of English soldiers shows that Flodden was no walkover, but the English did not lose leaders, members of the nobility or experienced military commanders, but four thousand dead from the conscripted levies from towns and villages of the northern counties left a mark for a generation.

You now have two options to return to the Monument car park. Either return along the Battlefield Trail, through the valley and turn right towards the

108

Monument, or continue along the road into Branxton village. The latter route takes you past "The Smallest Visitor Centre in the World", the old red phone box in the middle of Branxton. There is a small display here and Wi-Fi access to several websites will be available.

Turn left in the village and then take the left fork, past St Paul's Church. After the Battle the Church was used as a temporary mortuary. In Victorian times a bone pit was discovered when a new path to the Church was being constructed and it was assumed that this related to Flodden.

The Monument is visible from here and the car park is about 400 yards beyond the Church.

Stanley's Late Arrival

Although, as yet, there are no interpretation boards there is an extension to the original Battlefield trail which can be accessed as follows:

Go through the gate by the Scottish Battle Line board on Branxton Hill and continue eastward along the road to the small wooded area on the left. Through the gate, the path continues along the top of this field to the newly planted King James Wood.

Here, at the eastern end of Branxton Hill the last uncommitted Scottish Division waited for action. These were the free-ranging, hard-fighting Highlanders commanded by Earls Lennox and Argyll. They are armed, not with pikes, but with their traditional claymores and battle axes, but they wear little or no protective armour.   Discipline may not be their strong point, but, they are a formidable fighting force and may, even at this late stage, be able to change the course of the Battle.

From here the Highlanders can see that their King is in mortal danger, and rapidly they move to his rescue.

But just as the Highlanders are ready to move, Sir Edward Stanley arrives at the Battlefield along the crest of Branxton Hill, bringing his highly trained and experienced Cheshire and Lancashire archers.   His Division had left the overnight camp at Barmoor some time later than the main body of the English army, and came to Branxton by a different route.   Crossing the River Till near Etal or Ford, Stanley made his way through Sandyford, Crookham Dene and Pace Hill.

We do not know the reason for his late arrival at the Battle, but perhaps he had to make sure that Flodden Hill had been cleared of guns and soldiers before he could make his final approach. Another possibility is that Stanley was to guard the River Till and prevent the Scots retreating towards Berwick and away from the main English army.

With Stanley's flank attack, savage storms of arrows strike the Highlanders and, because they were only lightly armoured, cause carnage and heavy casualties. This surprise attack scatters the Highlanders and in the confusion many charge in disorder towards the mêlée of battle and block any possible line of retreat

From Branxton Hill To The Final Melee

The Death Of A King
It is believed that James IV died in battle near here

for King James.

The path continues down to the base of Branxton Hill, and through the line of trees in the valley. It then goes along the eastern, right hand edge of the next field. In all probability this is close to the route that James took as he fought his way towards the Earl of Surrey. If you stop as you approach the top of the Howard Ridge and look to your left towards the road close to the line of trees, you will see where we believe that King James IV of Scotland fell and became the last reigning Monarch to die in battle in the British Isles.

Go around the new Surrey Wood and then through the gate into the next field. Keep to the right around the edge of the field until you reach the field gate at the road that leads back into Branxton.

This last part of the Battlefield Trail takes you to where the Earl of Surrey would have made his final approach to the Battle. From here, looking south, you can see the crest of Branxton Hill and imagine the Scottish contingents lined up in readiness for the fight. You can also see that just to the north of Branxton there is another valley which, to this day, still fills with water after even moderate rain. It is still known as the Bog Field. Surrey must have felt that if the day went against him his chances of retreat were slim.

It would be about here that Surrey received the desperate message from his son Edmund begging for urgent reinforcements. It would have been from here that Surrey sent urgent instructions to Lord Dacre ordering him to ride to Edmund's beleaguered position. This single action probably did more than any other to change the course of the Battle of Flodden and, against the odds, gain victory for Surrey and for England.

The return to the Flodden car park is through Branxton. In the middle of the village you will find one of the old red phone boxes. This no longer has a public phone, but The Remembering Flodden Project has made it into perhaps the World's Smallest Visitor Centre! It now houses a map showing the routes of the two armies to war and has details of some local sites which are relevant to Flodden. It is intended that a public Wi-Fi hotspot will operate from here giving access to up to date websites of local interest.

Take the left fork at the Y junction at the western end of the village. You will pass St Paul's Church were it is said that bodies were taken after the Battle. St Paul's is well worth a visit. It is a Victorian rebuild, there remains a magnificent stone arch which dates back to Saxon times.

In Victorian times the then vicar, the Rev. Robert Jones, describes a bone pit which was discovered when a new path to the church was being made. Several bone pits are mentioned in publications and local folklore, but as this is being written, none have been recently found.

Many hope that this situation remains unchanged and that the "Brave of Both Nations" are left undisturbed.

The Road Around the Battlefield

Key:

1. Monument car park
2. Opening engagement
3. Dacre's arrival
4. Road to river crossing
5. Home & Huntly's line of advance
6. Assembly point for pike schiltron
7. View of King's chair
8. Road to south slope of Flodden Hill
9. View of Flodden Hill
10. View of Ford Castle
11. Direct route from Flodden Hill to Branxton Hill
12. Stanly's arrival
13. Surrey's arrival
14. Interpretation board
15. Interpretation board
16. View from Howard Ridge
17. Phone box visitor centre

The Road around the Battlefield

The action of the Battle of Flodden lasted for about four hours, and took place in the few fields as described above. The total battle front covered little more than a mile, and even then was confined to a maximum of four separate hand to hand conflicts each restricted to a front of a few hundred yards. But there is more to the story of this fateful Battle than the final clash of two opposing armies.

To appreciate the larger picture it is best to take to car or bicycle, and here we are fortunate in having a network of minor roads that allow good views of the Battlefield and the places that were so important in the lead up to the final conflict.

The road route starts at the Flodden Monument car park. Steps lead to the Monument where there is an excellent view of the Battlefield and an interpretation board that describes how the two armies were arrayed before the conflict.

Please be aware that many of the roads in north Northumberland are narrow and, this being an agricultural area, large tractors and trailers are often to be encountered, especially at harvest time. Please, at all times, drive with caution, and be aware that field gateways are regularly needed for access. Inconsiderate parking in field gateways or on the verge may cause obstruction to farm machinery and other essential road users.

Map 4 - The Road Around The Battlefield   115

The View of the Battlefield from the Road

(1.)

Starting from the Flodden Monument car park turn left (westwards) and drive through the small wooded area known as Dickie's Den. Almost immediately you cross a small stream, the Pallinsburn, which is said to have run red with blood for days after the Battle.

(2.)

Through the wooded area the road levels out onto to the flat land where, to the left, the first encounter took place. Cannon balls have been found in the fields around here, and a bone pit is marked on an early map. Local village folklore speaks of "The English bone pit" close to the road in this area. All this is evidence that here is where two opposing armies came into bitter and deadly contact.

The English approached the battlefield across a broad front from the north. The English Vanguard, commanded by Surrey's younger son, Edmund Howard, and the artillery train had crossed the River Till at Twizel Bridge, close to the Scottish Border. It is probable that they followed the road towards Cornhill on Tweed before swinging south to approach the battlefield through the fields where now stands a line of electricity pylons.

Edmund Howard's Vanguard is the first of the English Divisions into position and, as they arrive on the field

of battle, they find the Scots already arranged in four Divisions along the crest of Branxton Hill. There is opinion that the Scots, after hastily quitting their fortified position on Flodden hill, may well have been heading for the Tweed, home and safety. We do not know if this was the case and they were unfortunate to be caught in ambuscade, or if they were on Branxton Hill and already formed up in battle array. Some opinion has it that the Scottish Vanguard of Home and Huntly were indeed heading for the River Tweed, with orders to secure and guard a safe crossing point. If this were to be the case it at least part explains Home and Huntly's withdrawal from the field after their engagement with, and near rout of the English Vanguard. The fields to your left saw the first artillery exchange and it was here that Edmund Howard's Vanguard met the advancing pikes of Home and Huntly.

(3.)

To your right, along the line of pylons, is where Dacre's light cavalry galloped to Howard's rescue as his soldiers faltered, and began to run under the onslaught of Scottish pikes.

(4.)

Go to the road end, and at the T junction you meet a road which to the left climbs the western end of Flodden Hill and to the right heads to Learmouth, which 500 years ago was on the bank of the River Tweed and a known fording place. The river has, over the centuries, migrated northwards towards Coldstream. This is an ancient road and it appears on the earliest maps of the area. It would have been an obvious route for a Scottish withdrawal.

Turn left at the T junction and drive up the slope of Branxton Hill.

(5.)

Before you reach the electricity pylons there is an excellent view of the Battlefield. The Monument allows you to get your bearings and you can visualise the Scottish pike ranks moving into battle down the regular and gentle slope of the hillside, probably very close to line of pylons. There is no obstruction for the Scottish pikes to overcome before they engage with Howard's much smaller vanguard. It is also worth noting that you cannot see the eastern part of Branxton Hill and so cannot see the starting positions of the rest of the Scottish army.

Home and Huntly could not see, and could not have been seen, by their compatriots until they had joined in battle with the English Vanguard.

The Scottish pikes advanced in good order to the fields to the west of the Monument and soon beat back their English foes. Howard's Division had no answer to the massed ranks of pikes and their defences crumbled. In panic, English soldiers ran from the field. Many reports claim that they ran back to the north, away from immediate danger. The deserters then attacked

119

and looted their own baggage train which would have been trailing the Vanguard's advance and at some distance from the action.

From here you can see how Dacre could have galloped, unseen by the Scots, through the dead ground, the valley that runs north of Branxton and the Howard Ridge. Dacre would not have been seen by the Scots on Branxton Hill until he reached the flat open fields where the fighting was taking place. The pikes of the Scottish Centre would already be making their move and would have started down Branxton Hill to engage the Lord Admiral and his Division who by now were on the Howard Ridge near the Flodden Monument.

You can also understand from this position how it makes sense that Home did indeed leave the field to go and guard a crossing point of the Tweed. He would have expected that the pikes of the other Scottish Divisions would have similar success, and he believed that his priority was now to ensure that the prized and valuable Scottish guns could be moved to the safety of the northern banks of the Tweed. Home had no idea about the ground conditions further to the east in the valley at the foot of Branxton Hill. Nor did he have any idea about the full strength of the English army or the still distant Stanley contingent.

It was Dacre's timely arrival that not only saved Edmund Howard's life, but also stopped the flight of English soldiers from becoming a complete rout. Dacre's intervention not only halted the Scottish advance, but also prevented them from turning to

Flodden Monument

roll down towards the flank of the English Centre commanded by the Lord Admiral.

Drive to the top of the hill and continue to the road junction.

(6.)

On the flat fields behind the crest of Branxton Hill you can imagine the Scottish pikes being formed into schiltrons out of sight of the approaching English, but still being able to see and mark the enemy's progress.

(7.)

As you come to the junction you can see, just a little to the left of straight ahead, a wooded hill known as the King's Chair which is a continuation of Flodden Hill further to the left. We assume that the name of The King's Chair refers to the Scottish camp prior to the Battle. There is strong evidence, recently uncovered by a local archaeological group, of the presence of a Scottish camp on Flodden Hill and further work will continue over the coming years. An army of 28,000 soldiers would also probably include a similar number of non-combatants so the whole area of Flodden hill would have been a mass of closely packed people and activity.

When James realised that his artillery and defences faced the wrong direction, and that his battle plan had been thwarted, he had no option but to move his men, his guns and baggage train the mile and a half

Ford Castle and Flodden Hill
from the road near Branxton Moor Farm

Ford Castle

from Flodden Hill to the crest of Branxton Hill which is to your left and behind you. Moving the heavy guns would have been a slow and heavy task and the Scots would have struggled to have their artillery ready for use against the approaching English.

Turn left and drive as far as the farm.

(8.)

Here there is a right turn and this road takes you past the King's Chair to the south side of Flodden Hill where you can see the slope that was originally defended by the Scottish guns in anticipation of an English attack from Milfield Plain which lies directly in front of you. Return along the same road to point (8.)

(9.)

If you do not take this right turn, but continue ahead, to your right there is a good view of Flodden Hill where the Scots made their fortified and well defended camp as they awaited the arrival of Surrey' army.

(10.)

Move to the next left turn which is just a few hundred yards past the farm. From here you can just make out Ford Castle which is three miles directly ahead of you in the wooded area on the far side of the Till Valley. This was the last castle to be destroyed by the Scots before they set up their fortified position on Flodden Hill.

124

(11.)

Take the left turn.   It was over this ground that the Scots hauled their heavy guns as they rushed to defend the slopes of Branxton Hill.   Continue northwards, past the farm road to Branxton Hill Farm on the left, and proceed to the crest of Branxton Hill.

(12.)

On the right, through the field gate you can see to where Sir Edward Stanley and his Lancashire and Cheshire archers made their belated arrival along the top of the hill.   They had left Barmoor later than the main body of the English army, crossed the River Till near Ford or Etal and then made their way through Sandyford, Crookham Dene and Pace Hill.   It was in these fields, as the last uncommitted Scottish Division, the Highlanders of Lords Lennox and Argyll were starting their move to rescue King James in the valley to your front, that the Stanley's archers delivered the final blow against Scotland.

The Highlanders were caught in a flank attack and, in what was the last devastating arrow storm in battle from the English longbow, suffered grievous casualties, were scattered and were unable to save their King.

(13.)

Continue to the left hand corner to where the road turns down the slope of Branxton Hill.

From here, directly ahead, you can see where the Earl

of Surrey's Division formed up and then engaged in battle.

(14.)

At the next right hand bend you have a magnificent view of the Battlefield from close to King James' starting battle line.   The Battlefield Trail exits the field at this corner and there is an interpretation board just by the gate.

From here you can sense the dread feeling of the soldiers of King James' Division as they saw the Battle slipping away from them.   After the initial success of their Vanguard, the Scottish Centre Division was halted in the boggy ground at the foot of Branxton Hill. Their momentum lost, the pikes were now virtually useless, and the Scots had to face an onslaught of arrows from English archers before the billhooks commenced their bloody work.

The one chance for King James now is to kill or capture the English Commander, the Earl of Surrey. James can see from here that his Division outnumbers that of Surrey and if he moves quickly he has a chance to push home his attack before Surrey can be reinforced by soldiers from the English Centre. He has no idea that Stanley is very close and making his way along the crest of Branxton Hill, ready to make a devastating flank attack on the Highlanders.

It is about here that James made his fatal decision.

As he waited to engage in battle James would have seen his Centre Division, about a quarter mile to his left, march down the steep side of Branxton Hill. He would have seen how their progress was halted in the boggy ground at the foot of the slope and how his men suffered as here the pike proved no match for the billhook. But by now James' contingent was already committed to battle. From here you can see the steepness of the slope and, if you look to the field to the right of the road, you can also see that the contours are irregular, causing great variations in slope and ground conditions.

This is not good pike country.

(15.)

Make your way to the foot of Branxton Hill and note how, as you lose height, within a few yards, at the foot of the hill, the Howard Ridge looms in front of you. The valley is now drained by a drainage ditch, but five hundred years ago this area was a boggy morass, and it was the ground conditions, the topography and the terrain that were the key to victory or despair.

Imagine struggling through cloying mud, your compatriots slipping, falling and being crushed by following ranks of pikemen and then, after surviving arrow storms, being confronted by thousands of deadly billhooks. An interpretation board close to the road describes the final ferocious hand to hand fighting.

Close to this place King James fought his way towards

the banner of the Earl of Surrey. But the English Commander was well protected by his bodyguard. Here is where the final mêlée of the Battle of Flodden took place.

James' last hope of rescue by the intervention of the Highlanders does not materialise, and the confusion caused by Stanley's flank attack prevents any chance of retreat to Branxton Hill.

It was near here that King James IV of Scotland became the last Monarch to fall in battle in the British Isles. With their King, the heads and members of many Scottish noble and leading families also fell near here. In this valley the English billhook was dominant over the Scottish pike and the slaughter was horrific. Some 10,000 Scots and 4,000 English died within less than a mile of this place; a rate of slaughter that compares with some of the worst episodes on the Somme.

Drive up the slope of the Howard Ridge.

(16.)

From the top of the Ridge look towards Branxton Hill. You have a good view of the Scottish battle lines and from here you can imagine the fear and trepidation that engulfed the English as they made ready for battle.

The road now leads into Branxton.

Branxton Hill From The Howard Ridge
This photograph was taken after 2 days of summer rain

(17.)

In the middle of the village, you will find one of the old red phone boxes. This no longer has a public phone, but The Remembering Flodden Project has made it into perhaps the World's Smallest Visitor Centre! It now houses a map showing the routes of the two armies to war and has details of some local sites which are relevant to Flodden. It is intended that a public Wi-Fi hotspot will operate from here giving access to websites of local interest.

Turn left, and then take the left fork at the end of the village.

(18.)

This brings you to St Paul's Church where many bodies were taken after the Battle. St Paul's is well worth a visit. Although comprehensively rebuilt by the Victorians, there remains a magnificent stone arch which dates back to Saxon times.

The Flodden Monument car park (1.) is about 400 yards further along this road.

The Routes of the Two Armies to War

The Remembering Flodden Project has produced two detailed maps showing the routes of the two opposing armies as they drew inevitably to battle at Branxton. They give information about the known, and the probable places passed, river crossing points and why the armies took these particular routes.

Detailed directions along the quiet roads and byways keep you as close as possible to the lines of the armies' advance and are ideal for cyclists, walkers or to drive.

The maps are available as a set of two at local bookshops and Tourist Information Centres or from www.flodden.net.

Price £2.00 the pair.

The Route of the Scottish Army

This is 29 miles in total, but is divided into three almost equal sections.

Starting at Coldstream, the route follows the north bank of the Tweed, past Twizel Haugh, to Ladykirk and Norham Castle.

From here you move south to the River Till and Etal and Ford Castles.

Next the route takes you to Flodden Hill, Branxton Hill and the Battlefield.

The return includes Wark Castle and then across the River Tweed to Coldstream.

The Route of the English Army

This is also about 29 miles in total, and is divided into three sections.

Wooler is the start of this route and it goes across the River Till at Weetwood Bridge to Horton, and then along the old Roman road to Lowick and Barmoor.

From Barmoor you go along a series of minor roads, past Duddo Tower and again cross the River Till at Twizel Bridge. You then make your way southwards to Branxton and the Battlefield.

The return is over Flodden Hill to Milfield, and then across Milfield Plain to Doddington and Wooler.

An alternative route from Barmoor follows Stanley's probable approach to the Battle. From Barmoor head due west, past Ford Castle, and cross the River Till at Ford Bridge. It is uncertain where Stanley crossed the Till, but it was almost certainly between Ford and Etal. From the bridge, turn right towards Crookham, go through Sandyford, and cross the A697 close to the Blue Bell Inn, and head for Branxton.

The English Army at Flodden

The Vanguard

Commander: Edmund Howard
Approx. 3000 men

From
Cheshire, Macclesfield
Yorkshire, Doncaster, Hull.
Small contingent of Stanley's men from Lancashire
A few of the Lord Admiral's men

The Centre Division

Commander: The Lord Admiral
Approx. 9000 men

From
The Admiral's Fleet
Sir William Bulmer and Lord Lumley
commanding the
Bishop of Durham's retainers
and contingents from
Durham and Northumberland.
Lord Clifford's men from the Pennine Dales
Lord Conyers' men from Yorkshire. Sir Marmaduke
Constable and Sir William Percy
with men from Yorkshire and Northumberland
and others

The Rearguard

Commander: The Earl of Surrey
Approx 5000 men

Surrey's personal retinue
Lord Scrope, George Darcy men from Yorkshire,
East Riding
Swaledale, Wensleydale
York

Dacre's Horse

Commander: Lord Dacre
Approx.2000 men

From Cumberland, Westmorland, Northumberland
Also included other horse from
Tynemouth, Lancashire, Bamboroughshire

Sir Edward Stanley's Archers

Commander: Sir Edward Stanley
Approx 4000 men

Stanley tenants from
Lancashire and Cheshire

The Scottish Army at Flodden

The Vanguard

Commanders: Lord Home and the earl of Huntly
Approx 8000 men

Borderers from Berwickshire, Roxburghshire and the Merse.
Gordons and Highlanders from Inverness-shire and Aberdeenshire.

The Centre Division

Commanders: The Earls of Errol, Crawford and Montrose
Approx 6000 men

From Perthshire Angus, Forfar, Fife, and Scottish Lowlands

The Main Division

Commanded by King James IV
Approx. 9000 men

Royal Household troops
Earls of Cassillis, Morton and Rothes
Lords Herries, Maxwell, Innermeath,
Borthwick and Sempill
Men from Edinburgh, Ayr and Haddington
Galloway and Lowlands

The Highlanders

Commanders: Earls Lennox and Argyll
Approx. 6000 men

Highlanders – including Campbells, Macleans,
Mackenzies, Grants, MacDonalds
Men fromCaithness, Sutherland, Orkneys
Also the French military advisor,
Count d'Aussi and his 50 men-at-arms

Reserve Division

Commander: Earl of Bothwell
Approx. 4000 men

Lowland levies from the Lothians, Ettrick, Galashiels
and Selkirk

Artillery at Flodden

There is a great deal of confusion about the names, types and sizes of early artillery pieces.

A modern analogy can be found with names of models from the major car manufacturers. For example the Escort was introduced as Ford's small car. Over the years later models became more powerful and larger in size until a new small model, the Fiesta was introduced. Again subsequent models of the Fiesta increased in power and size, until the later Fiesta was larger and more powerful than earlier Escorts. The Escort was then dropped and replaced with a model called the Focus, and the Fiesta took the place of the Escort and was itself replaced by the Ka.

Similarly, types and sizes of artillery pieces changed and evolved over time. Add to this the fact that the standardisation of measurement of weight and length did not come in until the late 1500s, and the difficulties of comparing and quantifying the different types of artillery pieces become obvious.

At Flodden the artillery pieces used covered the full range of types made at the time. The 5 Cannon and 2 Culverin of the Scottish artillery train were known as the Seven Sisters and were amongst the largest guns in the British Isles. To move these heavy guns, each needed a team of 36 oxen, a lead horse, 9 drivers and about twenty workmen. This compares to the light English Falconet which was light enough to be man-hauled.

The light English guns fired a small ball which, compared to the heavy Scottish guns, had a very high muzzle velocity, and in field combat, were much more effective weapons. In contrast, the heavy Scottish guns were designed for siege use and battering down walls and masonry where the time taken to do so was not the primary consideration.

Artillery at Flodden

Type	Number	Bore	Weight of Shot	Weight of Piece	Max Range
		inches	lbs	lbs	yards
The Scottish Guns					
Cannon	5	8	60	8000	3000
Culverin	2	5.5	20	4500	3000
Culverin Pickmoyen	4	4	7	2800	2800
Culverin Moyen	6	2.5	3	1500	2800
The English Guns					
Serpentine	5	3.75	5	1500	2500
Falconet	18	2	1	500	1500

Fig 3

Flodden Timeline - The Countdown to War

English Events	Date	Scottish Events	
Henry VIII embarks for France. Earl of Surrey made Lord Leiutenant of the Northern Marches. Surrey organises supplies and his personal retinue of 500	1513 Late June		F-77
Henry arrives in Calais with army of southern levies and all the best kit	30 June		F-71
Grain supplies arrive in Newcastle	12 July		F-59
	19 July	James IV orders his fleet to be ready for action	F-52
Henry ready to march on Therouanne	21 July		F-50
	24 July	Feudal host assembled at Edinburgh. All men 16-60 to be ready within 20 days with 40 days provision	F-47

Fig 4

142

	25 July	Scottish fleet sails	F-76
	26 July	Lyon Herald sent to Henry in France with declaration of war	F-45
	11 Aug	Lyon Herald arrives at Therouanne to deliver ultimatum	F-29
	13 Aug	The Ill Raid. Home defeated at Milfield	F-27
Battle of the Spurs. Henry's army drives off French cavalry at Therouanne	16 Aug		F-24
Dacre writes to Bishop of Durham suggesting buying off the Scots.	17 Aug		F-23
	19 Aug	Scots mustered at Edinburgh ready to march	F-21
	21 Aug	Scots Army past the Lammermuirs	F-19

English Events	Date	Scottish Events	
	22 Aug	Scots ford River Tweed and enter England	F-18
	24 Aug	James holds his last parliment at Twizel	F-16
At Pontefract Surrey hears of Scottish invasion	25 Aug		F-15
English march York to Durham			
	29 Aug	Norham Castle taken by Scots. More provisions arrive	F-11
Surrey arrives in Newcastle	30 Aug		F-10
Englsih army leaves Newcastle	31 Aug		F-9
	1 Sept	Ford Castle taken by Scots. Camp on Flodden Hill. James now waits for Surrey	F-8
Surrey arrives at Bolton, Alnwick	3 Sept		F-6
Full muster at Bolton. Lord Admiral arrives, Supplies until 9th Sept	4 Sept		F-5

English actions	Date	James actions	
	5 Sept	James leaves and burns Ford Castle. Joins camp on Flodden Hill	F-4
Herald Rouge Croix sent to James with offer of battle on 9th - No Quarter	5 Sept	Rouge Croix detained by James but Herald Islay sent with agreement to battle	F-4
English move to Wooler Haugh. Surrey expects to fight on Milfield Plain	6 Sept		F-3
Rouge Croix returns to Surrey with news of fortifications on Flodden Hill	7 Sept		F-2
Surrey moves to Barmoor	8 Sept	James now unsure of Surrey's intentions.	F-1
English army move via Duddo and Twizel to approach Branxton from the north	9 Sept	James moves hurriedly to defend the high ground of Branxton Hill	F-Day

Battle Joined at 4pm

A Few "What ifs"

What if the Battle had been fought on Milfield Plain?

The outcome of the Battle of Flodden was not a foregone conclusion and the day might well have gone for Scotland if circumstances and events had been slightly different.

In spite of his early preparations for war, the Earl of Surrey was desperately working to match King James' mobilisation. The English army had to be raised as it marched north and the Scots, already established as invaders on English soil, had scoured the land for supplies and forage, forcing the English to rely entirely on the provisions they carried with them. This limited quantity of supplies meant that Surrey's options for Battle were extremely limited.

As the English mustered at Bolton near Alnwick the two armies were close enough for the formalities to begin and for Battle to be arranged. Surrey sent his Herald to offer Battle on September 9th, the last day his supply situation would allow. James agreed to this, but held Surrey's Herald prisoner and sent his reply by his own Herald, thus preventing intelligence about the Scottish position on Flodden Hill falling into English hands.

After securing his chosen date for battle, Surrey moved his army to Wooler, about eight miles from the Scottish camp. Surrey had expected to fight on the "flat fair land" of Milfield Plain, but was perhaps unaware of the number of Scottish pikes he would have to face. When his Herald finally returned with news of the Scottish guns and fortifications on Flodden Hill, Surrey immediately sent him back with entreaties for the Scots to abandon their advantageous position and engage in battle on Milfield Plain. James would not listen; he refused to leave Flodden Hill and made it clear that he, a King, would take no orders from a "mere Earl".

However, if James had accepted this challenge, his pikes may well have had the advantage on the flat ground of Milfield Plain and Surrey's archers and billhooks may not have been the answer to steady rolling schiltrons of pikes.

What if Surrey had attacked Flodden Hill?

The next problem that Surrey had to address was where to attack. He now knew that the southern slope of Flodden Hill was defended by guns, and to attack here would be suicidal. He had to find another line of attack, or a way to dislodge the Scots from the security of their defensive position.

Surrey had as a scout, The Bastard Heron, an outlaw, but one who knew the lie of the local land intimately. The Bastard Heron advised of a route to outflank the Scottish position on Branxton Hill, and Surrey made his vital decision which, at a stroke, changed the whole strategic situation. By taking this advice and moving the army to Barmoor, James no longer could be certain of Surrey's intentions. Were the English going to attack? Were they going to wait for supplies from the now accessible port of Berwick? Or were they going to cross the River Tweed and advance to the undefended Scottish capital of Edinburgh?

Even if Surrey did nothing more, the Scottish position on Flodden Hill was now untenable. If Surrey had not moved from Wooler, or had made directly for Flodden Hill, the outcome of the Battle would probably have been very different.

What if the English had arrived at Branxton earlier or later?

This is a matter of timing. As the English finally advanced from the north towards Branxton Hill they found the Scots already in battle array along the crest of the hill. We do not know if the Scots had moved here to defend the high ground, or if they were making a strategic withdrawal back across the Tweed. If the latter was the case then Surrey's timing was indeed fortunate. An hour later and the Scots would have been in the safety of their homeland. An hour earlier, if the Scots had been close to, but not yet visible on the crest of Branxton Hill, the English may well have been caught as they climbed the steep northern slopes into lines of pikes and an easily defended Scottish position.

The difference of an hour either way of the English advance would have meant that the opening positions of the battle were entirely different; or might not have existed at all, and the Battle of Flodden might never have been fought.

What if the Scots had stayed on Branxton Hill?

If the Scots had held their position on Branxton Hill and the English had attacked, the outcome of the Battle of Flodden would have been very different. If the English had attacked, they would first have had to make their way through the marshy valley, and they would have suffered the same cloying mud that hampered the Scots' progress. They would then have had to face the exhausting climb up the steep northern slope of Branxton Hill. At the top they would have come up against an impenetrable line of Scottish pikes. The longbows of the English archers would have had a greatly reduced effect because they would have been shooting uphill, and their arrows would consequently lose some of their energy and killing force.

Used in defence, the back of the pikes would be stuck into the ground, and the weapons held at an angle so that they presented an array of spear points to the attacker. The Scots had superior numbers, and the English would have had little chance in hand to hand fighting, especially as the Scots would have held the higher ground. It is uncertain where the Scottish guns would have been, but if any guns were in place they would have added severely to English difficulties.

Had the Scots stayed on Branxton Hill there may well have been a stand off or stalemate, but the possibility of an English victory would have been extremely remote.

What if Home and Huntly had stayed on the Battlefield?

Home and Huntly left the field after their attack on Edmund Howard's Vanguard. Why? We cannot be sure, but there is opinion that this Scottish Division had been ordered to secure and guard a crossing point over the River Tweed.

After Dacre's rescue mission Home and Huntly did leave the field and it will always be open to speculation as to what might have happened if the 8000 Scots had regrouped and moved down the English flank to catch the Lord Admiral's Centre Division in a pincer movement as the Scottish Centre moved into action down Branxton Hill.

What if the Scots had not used pikes?

The Scots were perhaps too ambitious in adopting the pike as their main attack weapon. Pikes needed tight formation, competent drill and, most of all, strict discipline. The Scots had only a few weeks to train to use pikes and when they were brought to action the topography and the ground conditions were against them. Perhaps commanders more experienced in the use of pike would have realised these difficulties and either, relied on the more traditional sword and battleaxe, or else avoided battle altogether.

What if Surrey had lost?

James had already fulfilled his promise to take "one yard of English land" and may have returned to Scotland, probably taking possession of Berwick-upon Tweed as he did so. He may have had plans to venture further south into England, but had he done so he would soon have come across a further English army which had been gathered together by Catherine of Aragon and was already marching northwards to support Surrey.

What if James had reached and killed the Earl of Surrey?

The death or capture of the Earl of Surrey would have dealt a devastating blow to English morale, but it is quite possible that Surrey's elder son, the Lord Admiral would have moved to take immediate control of the army and that the final outcome of Flodden remained the same.

1513 Country

The story of the Battle of Flodden encompasses much more than the few fields over which the Battle was fought. The following is a list of places that are part of that wider story. More information is available on www.flodden.net

In or near Branxton:

Flodden Battlefield
400yds west of TD12 4SN - The site of the Battle.

St. Paul's Church
TD12 4SN - Where bodies were taken after the Battle.

Marmion's Well
100yds north of TD12 4SN. On the riverside below St. Paul's Church - A site central to Sir Walter Scott's epic poem.

Branx Brig
TD12 4SJ - Where some of the advancing English are said to have crossed the Palinsburn stream. There is a footpath from the Inch Cottage, between Branxton and Crookham.

Branxton Hill
TD12 4QF - Where the Scots lined up for battle.

Flodden Hill
TD12 4TF. One mile south of Branxton - The site of the Scottish camp as they awaited the arrival of Surrey and his army.

In or near Crookham:

Sandyford
TD12 4TH. Just east of Crookham village - Mentioned
in early texts as being on Stanley's route to the Battle.

Crookham Dene
TD12 4TD. To the west of Crookham - Mentioned in
early texts as being on Stanley's route to the Battle.

Pace Hill
300 yards south of TD12 4TD at the eastern end of
Branxton Hill - Mentioned in early texts as being on
Stanley's route to the Battle.

In or near Coldstream:

Coldstream Museum
TD12 4BD - Close to the site of a Cistercian Priory
whose nuns tended the wounded after the Battle.
Telephone 01890 882630.

Coldstream Church
TD12 4DL Coldstream High Street - Here there is a
window dedicated to Scots who died at Flodden.

Priory Monument
TD12 4BB - A recent monument on Tweed Green, the
work of the Flodden 1513 Club.

In or near Ford and Etal

Ford Castle (not open to the public)
TD12 4PX - Taken and burned by the Scots on route to
Flodden Hill.

Etal Castle
TD15 4 TN - Captured by the Scots on route to
Flodden Hill. English Heritage museum and Flodden
exhibition.

Medieval Bridge, Etal
300 yards south of TD15 4TN. Close to the Etal end
of Heatherslaw Light Railway - Perhaps used to bring
the captured Scottish guns to Etal Castle.

Heatherslaw Corn Mill
TD12 4TJ - A mill has existed here since before the
Battle of Flodden.

Further Afield

Wark Castle
TD12 4RG - The first castle to be taken by the Scots as
they invaded England.

Twizel Bridge
TD12 4UX - Built in 1511, the English Vanguard and
artillery used this bridge on their way to battle.

Twizel Haugh
South bank of the Tweed to the west of Twizel Bridge.
King James held his last Parliament here.

Barmoor Castle
TD15 2TR - The site of the English camp on the night
before the Battle.

Flodden Gates
TD15 2TR - Magnificent gates recently erected as a
Flodden Memorial at the entrance to Barmoor Castle.

Milfield Plain
NE71 6HR - Site of the "Ill raid" just before Flodden.
Surrey had expected to fight on this flat ground.

Norham Castle
TD15 2JY - Heavily defended but taken by the Scots
after siege and artillery barrage.

Ladykirk Church
TD15 1XL - Built by King James after nearly
drowning in the Tweed.

Wooler Haugh
NE71 6NJ - Site of the English camp prior to their
moving to Barmoor.

Surrey House
NE71 6QS, A697 1.5 miles south of Wooler - A decrepit
and disgracefully neglected house on the site where
Surrey is reputed to have stayed on his way to
Flodden.

Wooler Tower
NE71 6LH - Mentioned in 1509 as a defensive tower
with a garrison of 20 soldiers. Church street Wooler.

Weetwood Bridge
NE71 6EX - The English army crossed the River till around here on their outflanking move to Barmoor.

Berwick upon Tweed
TD15 - Avoided by the Scots on their advance, but became a possible lifeline for supplies for the English after their move to Barmoor.

Bolton, Alnwick
NE66 - The final muster point for the English army. Surrey met his son, the Lord Admiral here.

Ellem Ford
TD11 3SG - Ellem Ford Church. King James is reputed to have seen a spectre warning him against military action.

Flodden Wall, Edinburgh
EH8 9UA - Built after Flodden as belated defences in case the English should attack Edinburgh.

Fletcher Monument, Selkirk
TD7 4JY - Commemorates the sole survivor of Selkirk men who fought at Flodden, and the capture of the Macclesfield banner.

Middleton Church, Manchester
M24 6DJ - This magnificent 15th century Church
houses stained glass windows depicting twelve
archers who fought at Flodden.

Arncliffe Church, North Yorks.
BD23 5QE - The names of local men who came to
Flodden are displayed here as is an example of an
English billhook.

Mary Rose Museum, Portsmouth
PO1 3LX - The Mary Rose was the Lord Admirals
flagship and brought him to Newcastle at the head of
a supply fleet.

Other walks in 1513 Country

There is a public footpath over Flodden Hill. A track runs from the ruined cottages at the roadside close to Blinkbonny Farm on the northern edge of Flodden Hill, and goes through the wooded area, round the top of the hill and then cuts southwards to the hamlet of Flodden. It then continues to Milfield Hill which is just north of the village of Milfield.

This path takes you close to the Scottish camp on Flodden Hill. You can imagine where the heavy guns might have been emplaced on the southern slopes to guard against an English attack from Milfield Plain. As you walk down here you realise that an attack by the English as they climbed these slopes into heavy gunfire would have been suicidal, and that Surrey's only option was to find another way of dislodging the Scots from this strongly fortified position.

Through the trees Ford Castle can be seen, as can Branxton Hill and the ground over which the heavy guns had to be dragged to defend against the unexpected English attack from the north.

This track over Flodden Hill is part of a longer footpath route that originates at Etal, and goes along the River Till, through Crookham, Crookham Dene and Pace Hill to the ruined cottages at Blinkbonny. These rights of way are marked on OS Explorer Map 339, but in places are better marked on the map than they are on the ground.

New paths are planned and will be opened in the near future. These will be publicised as soon as there are opened to the public.

Maps will be available to download from the Remembering Flodden Project's website, www.flodden.net

Other Battlefields in the Borderlands

Lindisfarne   c590
Degsastan (Dawston Rigg)   603
Carham I   833
Carham II   1018
Alnwick I   1093
Alnwick II   1174
Dunbar I   1296
Halidon Hill   1333
Neville's Cross   1346
Otterburn   1388
Homildon Hill   1402
Nesbit Moor   1402
Yeavering   1415
Piper Dene   1435
Hexham I   1463
Hedgeley Moor   1464
Hexham II   1464
Milfield (The Ill raid) 1513
Flodden   1513
Melrose   1526
Hadden Rigg   1542
Solway Moss   1542
Hadden Rigg   1542
Ancrum Moor   1545
Pinkie   1547
Grindon Rigg   1558
Carberry Hill   1567
Langside   1568
Haydon Bridge   1587

Newburn   1640
Newcastle   1644
Philiphaugh   1645
Dunbar II   1650
The Crookham Affray 1678
Prestonpans   1745
Rullion Green   1666

Details on the above can be found on The Battlefields Trust website www.battlefieldstrust.com and in Cassell's Battlefields of Britain and Ireland.

Note: The Town of Berwick-upon-Tweed can be described as a battlefield itself, and perhaps one of the longest lasting battlefields. In less than five hundred years Berwick changed hands between the English and Scots on thirteen occasions. These changes were the result of local battles, sieges or financial transactions, and the importance of Berwick as a strategic Border town is marked by the existence of a castle and at least two sets of defensive walls.

20th Century

There are numerous 20th Century battlefield related sites in the Borders. These include practice WWI trenches at Otterburn, and lines of WWII defensive pillboxes along the coast and further inland. There are several WWII airfields, including Milfield, Eshott and Charterhall and it is possible to find remnants of a POW camp at Wooler.

Numerous crash sites of aircraft, both allied and attacking, have been noted in the Borders, and an enigmatic line of gravestones in Kirknewton Churchyard marks the final resting places of young pilots and aircrew.

Evidence of a troubled past in the Borders is found in the number of castles and fortifications that remain. There are two walled towns, Berwick-upon-Tweed and Alnwick and probably more castles per square mile that any where else in the Western World. Nearly every town, village and settlement in the Borders has its Tower, Bastle, or fortified house.

Details of these sites are being compiled and lists of Castles, Towers, Bastles, Walled towns, Fortified houses will soon be made available on a new website: www.northumberlandsecrets.co.uk.

Further Reading

Although many histories of Flodden have been written, most if not, all are currently out of print. Some will be re-issued, and new books will be published in the coming months.

The following list is not comprehensive, but these books, or facsimile reprints, are available if you look around.

We will try to keep a full and up to date bibliography on www.flodden.net

Barr N.   Flodden (2001)

Barr N   Flodden 1513 The Scottish Invasion of Henry VIII's England   (2001)

Bell J D   From Boroughmuir to Branxton - The Story of Flodden (2004)

Elliot F   The Battle of Flodden and raids of 1513 (1911)

Jones R   The Battle of Flodden Field fought September 9th 1513 (1864)

Kightly C   Flodden The Anglo-Scottish War of 1513 (1975)

Leather G F T   New Light on Flodden (1937)

Mackenzie W M   The Secret of Flodden (1931)

Reese P   Flodden a Scottish Tragedy (2003)

Sadler J   Flodden 1513 Scotland's Greatest
Defeat (2006)

White R   The Battle of Flodden Fought 9 Sept
1513 (1859)

FATAL RIVALRY: Flodden 1513 - Power, Personality and the Decisive Battle for Renaissance Britain by George Goodwin. Publication by Weidenfeld & Nicolson, £20, Spring 2013 – www.georgegoodwin. com. Gives the historical background leading to the battle and brings alive the extraordinary personalities involved including Kings Henry VIII and James IV and their Queens Katherine of Aragon and Margaret Tudor. By the author of the acclaimed Fatal Colours: Towton 1461.

Larger versions of the maps used in this book are available to download from The Remembering Flodden Project's website www.flodden.net. Up to date information about Flodden, the Battlefield and related topics and events can be found on this website.

The following websites show other places of interest in north Northumberland and the Borders:

www.northumberlandsecrets.co.uk

www.thisisnorthumberland.com

Remembering Flodden: www.flodden.net

Shops, Pubs and Cafés in the Area

Cornhill Village Shop and Coffee Shop, Cornhill on Tweed, TD12 4UH
t.01890 883313
www.cornhillvillageshop.co.uk

The Collingwood Arms,Cornhill on Tweed, TD12 4UH
t.01890 882424
www.collingwoodarms.com

The Blue Bell, Crookham, TD12 4SH
t. 01890 820789
www.bluebellcrookham.co.uk

The Red Lion Inn, Milfield, NE71 6JD
t. 01668 216224
www.redlionmilfield.co.uk

Café Maelmin, Milfield, NE71 6JD
t.01668 216323

Milfield General Store, Milfield, NE71 6JD
t.01668 216281

Ford Shop & Post Office, Ford, TD15 2QG
t.01890 820230
email. fordvillageshop.aol.com

The Old Dairy, Ford, TD15 2PX
t.01890 820325
www.theolddairyinford.co.uk

Heatherslaw Tea Room, Heatherslaw, TD12 4TJ
t.01890 820737
kathleencockburn@rocketmail.com

The Black Bull, Etal, TD12 4TL
t.01890 820200
www.ford-and-etal.co.uk

Lavender Tearooms, Etal, TD12 4TN
t.01890 820777
www.thelavendertearooms.org.uk

The Fenton Centre, Fenton, NE71 6JL
t.01668216216
http://www.fentoncentre.com

There are several shops, pubs and cafés in each of the larger villages and towns of: Coldstream, Norham, Lowick, Wooler, Berwick-upon-Tweed, and Kelso.